# Serial Killers Coloring Book

## by

## Kitty Belle

**Copyright © 2020 Kitty Belle**

All rights reserved.

No part of this book may be reproduced in any form or by any electronic or mechanical means including information storage and retrieval systems without written permission from the author, except for the use of brief quotations in a book review.

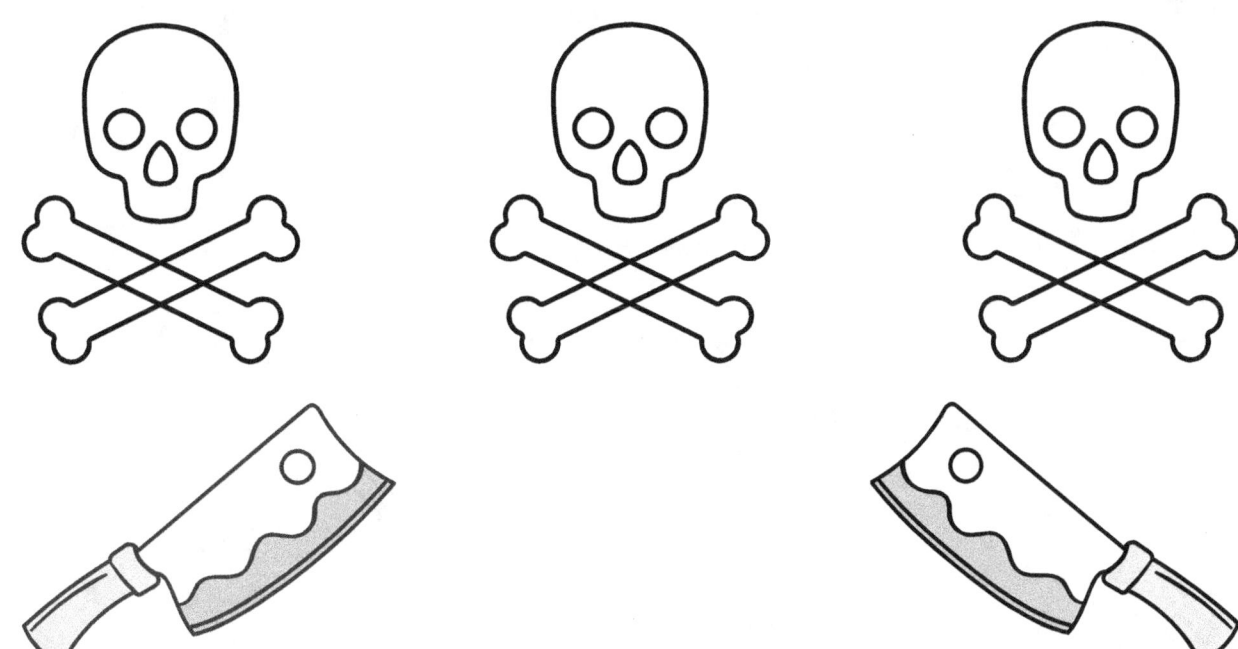

# This serial killers coloring book belongs to:

.............................

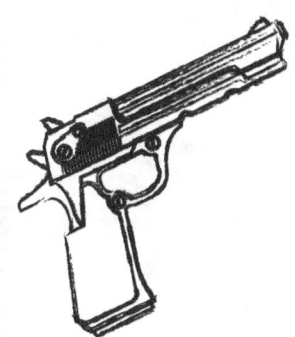 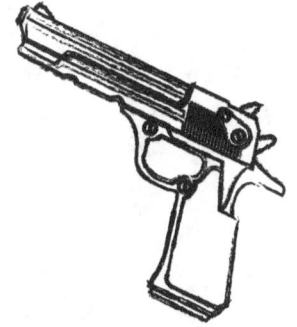

# Introduction

Hello and welcome to a coloring book with a difference. You're not going to find any rainbow colored unicorns, or soft and cute little kittens here, sorry. It's quite the opposite in fact. Here we have an A to Z of the world's most notorious deranged male serial killers.

So, what makes a serial killer? What are their modi operandi? What is it that fuels their desire to service their abnormal psychological gratification? Well, serial killers can be classified into four main groups depending on the nature and characteristics of their crimes. There are also 'organized' and 'disorganized' killers. Organized killers have a tendency to be graced with higher intelligence levels with every element of their gruesome crimes meticulously planned out well in advance to ensure that there can be no chance of leaving any evidence that may incriminate them. Is it often the case that these organized killers can stalk their victims for weeks, or even months in advance of their crimes to increase the chance of 'perfecting' their attacks. Disorganized killers, on the other hand, typically kill at random with little or no pre-planning. Their victims are, more often than not, in the wrong place at the wrong time. It's also a trait of such a killer to be of no fixed abode and they move from state to state or even flee to other countries to escape detection.

So, the first main 'type' of serial killer is the 'thrill seeker'. These killers consider their misdemeanours to be some sort of wild and convoluted game with the authorities. Sometimes they can even turn up or be near the aftermath of their killings to watch and observe from a distance. They typically maintain and store detailed records of their crimes. Thrill seekers mostly use weapons to attack their victims and often rape their victims before (or sometimes after) killing them. They then discreetly dispose of the body so they can start to plan the next trill seeking mission.

There's also those that seek 'Power and Control' over their victims. They get enjoyment from the misery of their victims, possibly due to having been victims themselves from abusive parents or carers leaving them powerless and with considerable feelings of inadequacy. Again, this type of killer usually rapes his victims, not for sexual gratification specifically, but for the feeling of domination that they may gain from it.

'Mission oriented' serial killers feel that they are giving something back to society or doing society a favor. The victims are typically sex workers, drug dealers, homosexuals or people that the killers think shouldn't form part of society. Their actions, to them, are considered to a societal cleansing ritual. These mission-oriented killers don't tend to be psychotic and they always have a controlled manner in which they execute their crimes, thus making them slightly easier to learn what their next move might possibly be.

Finally, there are 'Visionary Serial Killers'. This last killer type sometimes feel that they are compelled to their crimes through higher powers such as God or the Devil. They are killers who suffer psychotic breaks from the society in which

surrounds them. They believe their actions aren't of their own doing and they are very detached from reality.

Perhaps you can try and work out what category each of these killers fall into as you complete the book?

There are many more subcategories of serial killers, but this isn't a book designed to psychologically analyze each serial killer. This book is here for you to learn a little about their atrocious crimes and gruesome stories while also gaining some knowledge on why these killers consider their work to be more than just killings. For many, they consider their crimes to be 'art'. Each killer is intricately drawn and includes content that is relevant and contextual to their villainous and terrible crimes.

So, we now know about their 'art', let's enjoy *our* art by bringing to life this selection of the world's most notorious and deranged serial killers with your color and imagination.

Enjoy and have fun,

Kitty B

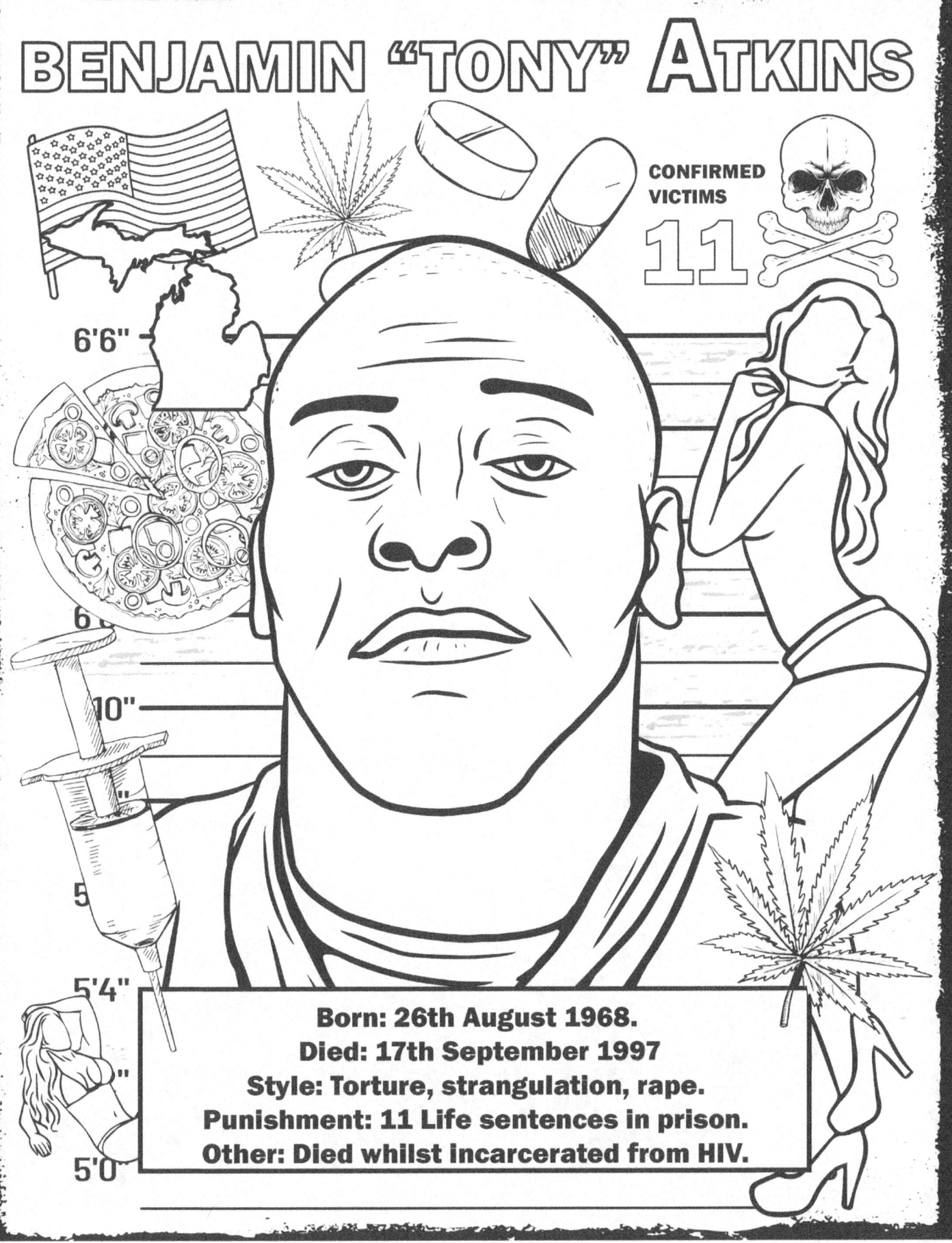

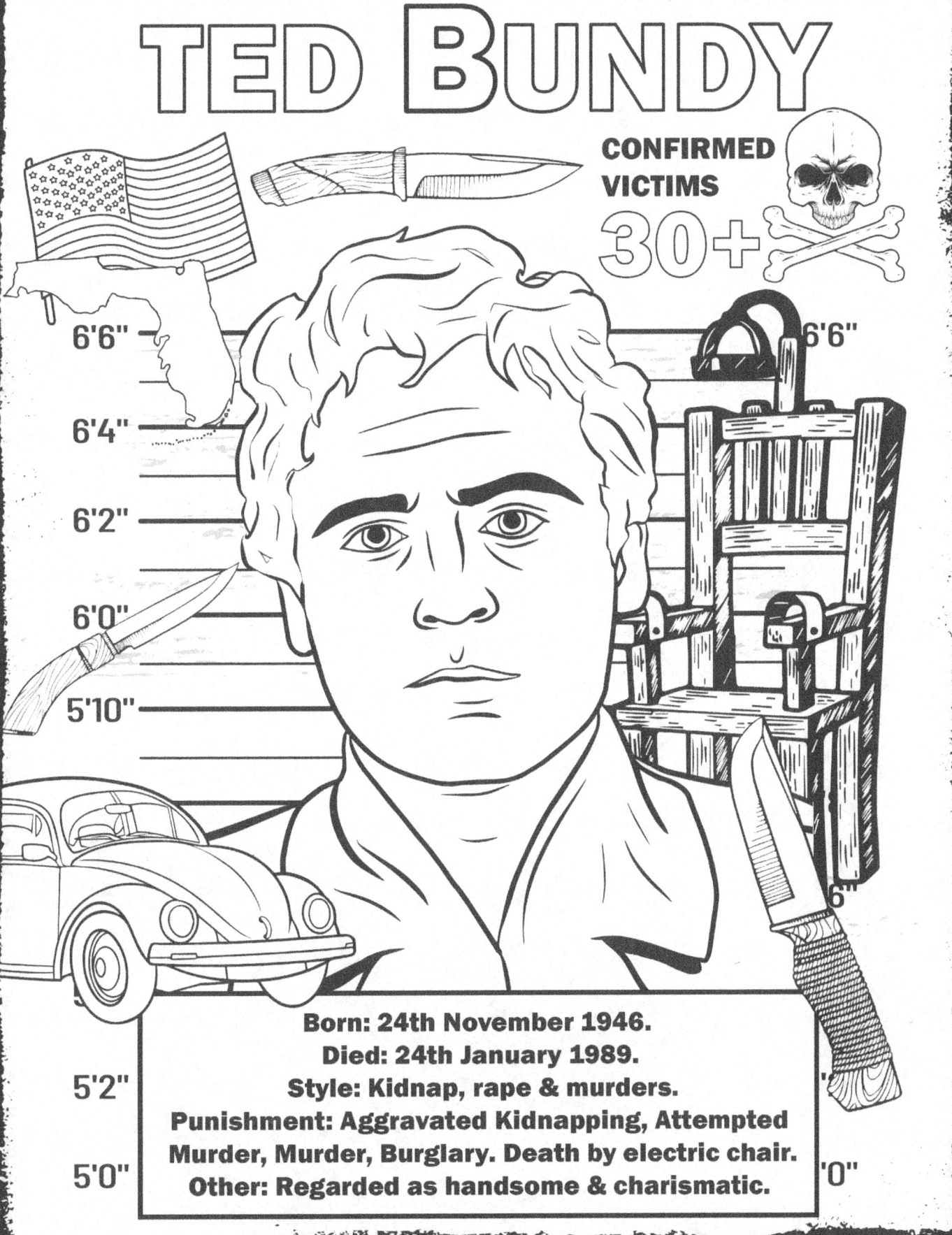

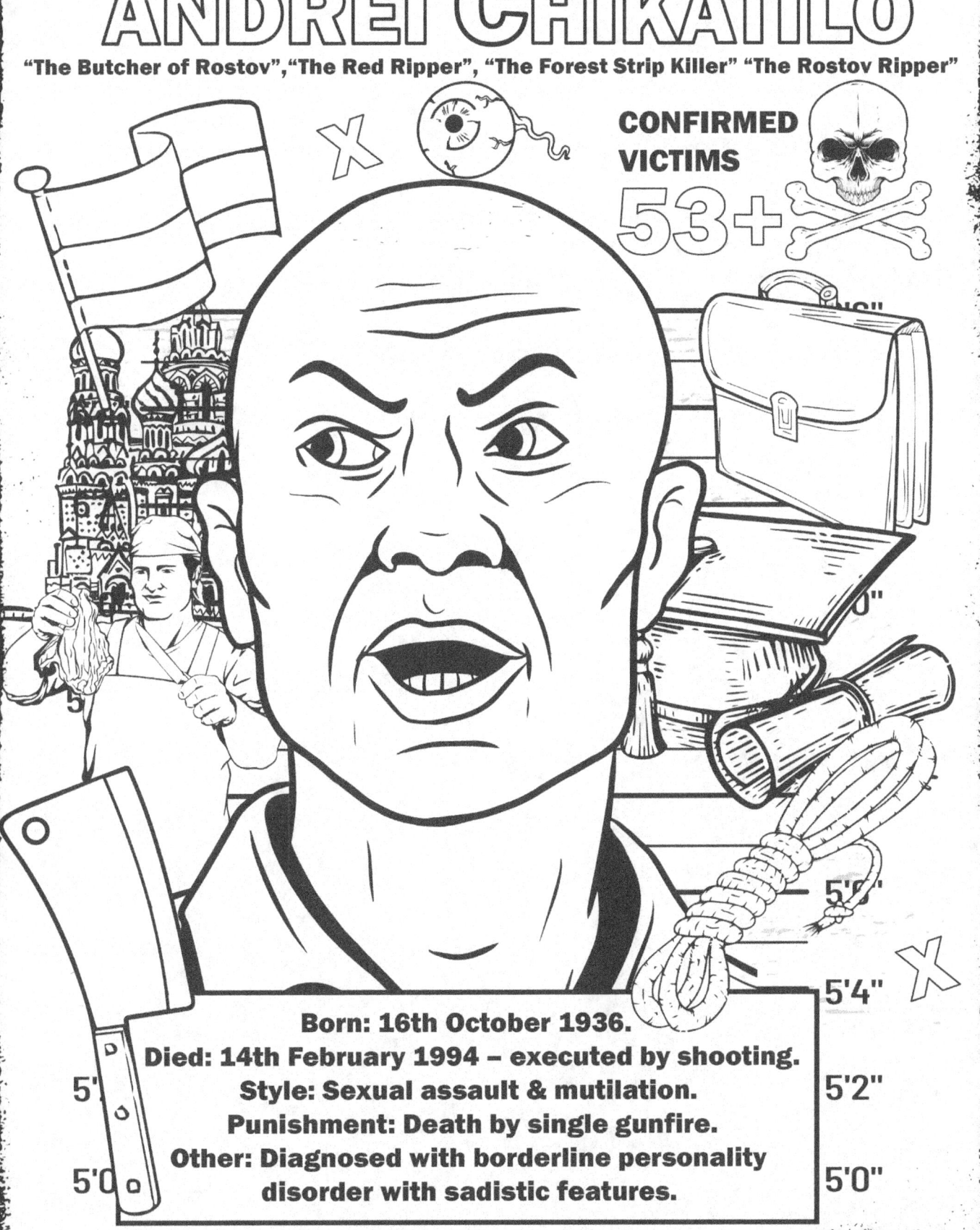

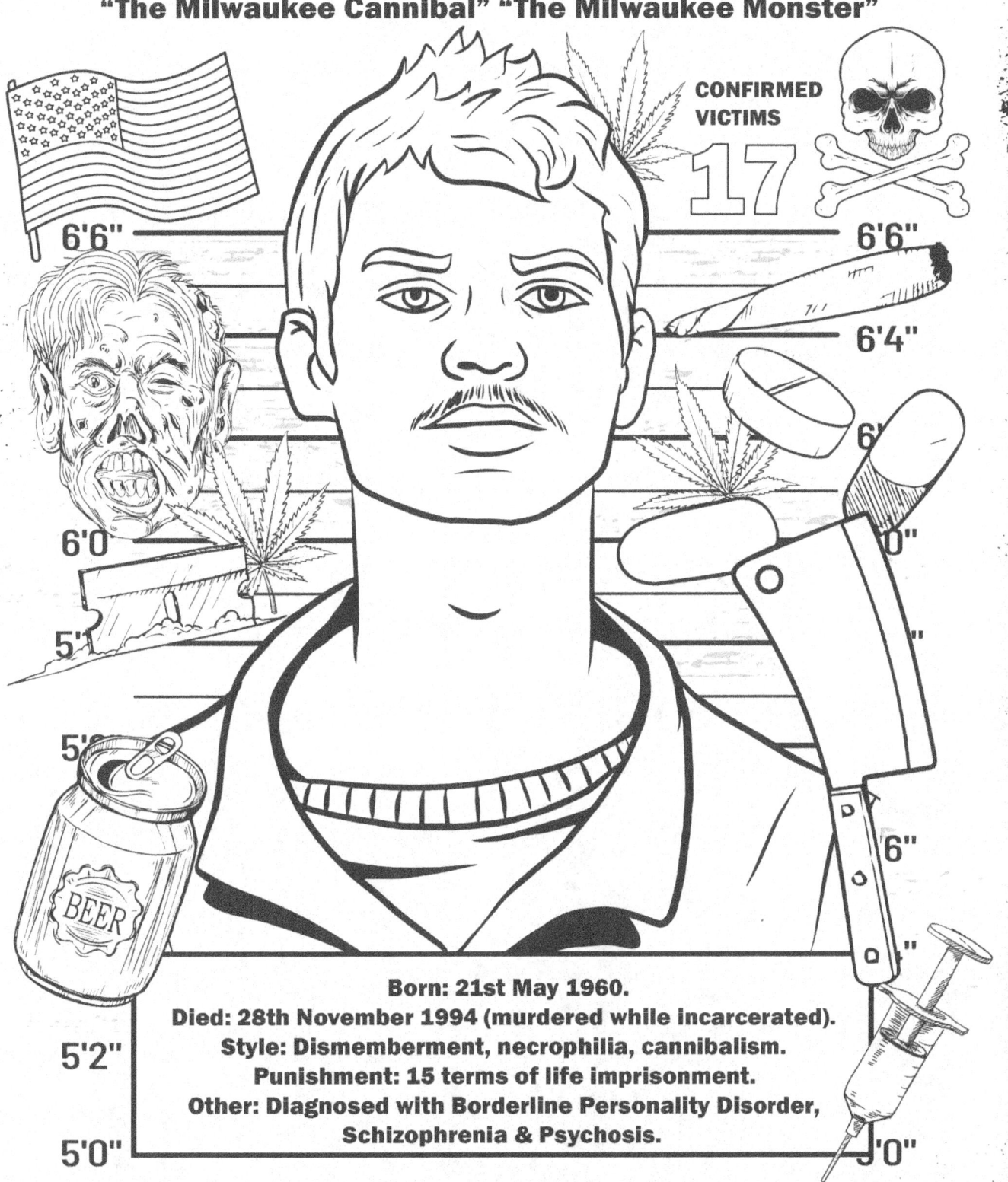

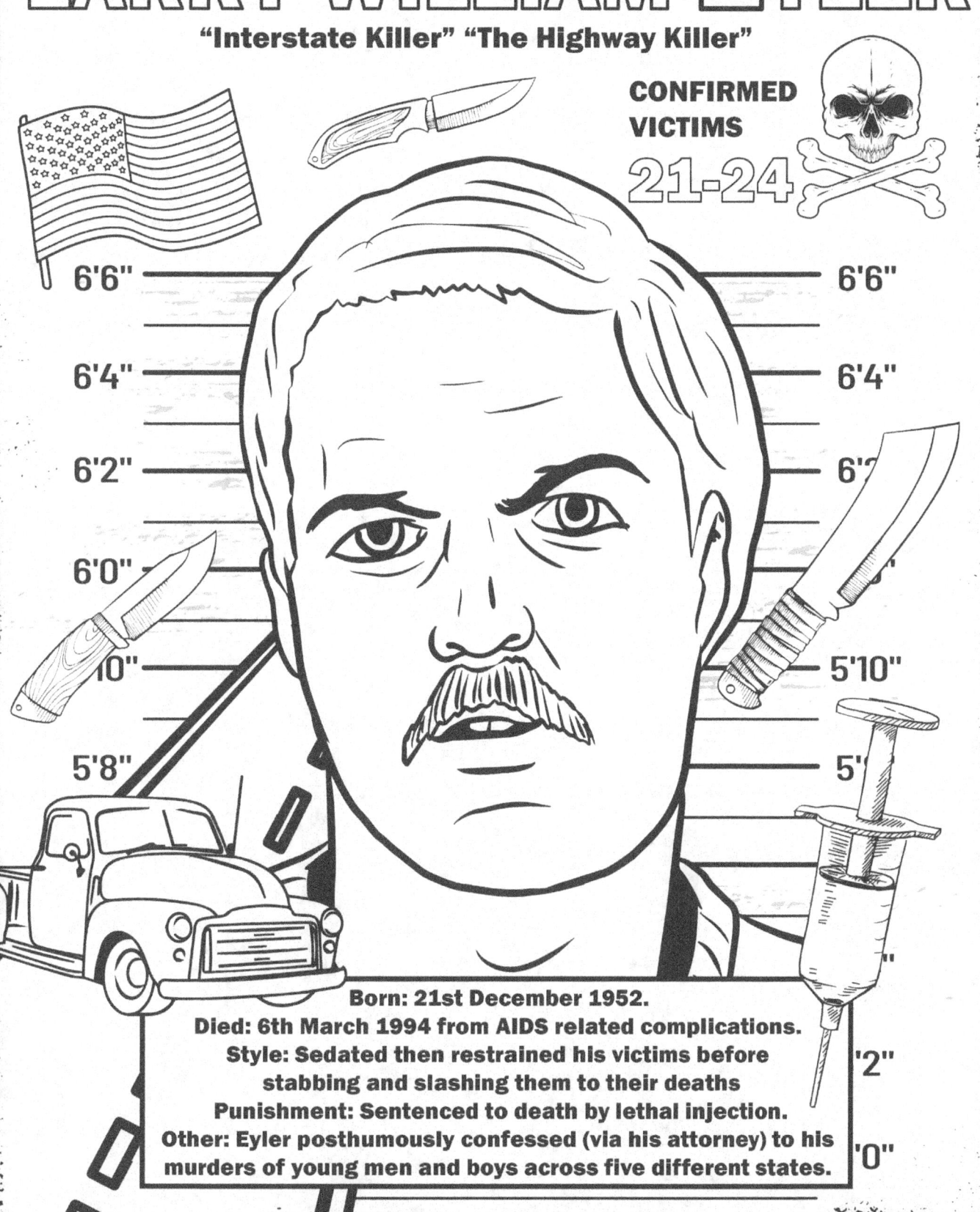

# ALBERT FISH

"The Grey Man" "Werewolf of Wysteria" "Brooklyn Vampire".
"Moon Maniac" "The Boogey Man"

**CONFIRMED VICTIMS**
**3**
(although possibly 100+)

Born: 19th May 1870.
Died: 16th January 1936.
Style: Kidnap and murdering.
Punishment: Death by electric chair.
Other: A known bigamist.

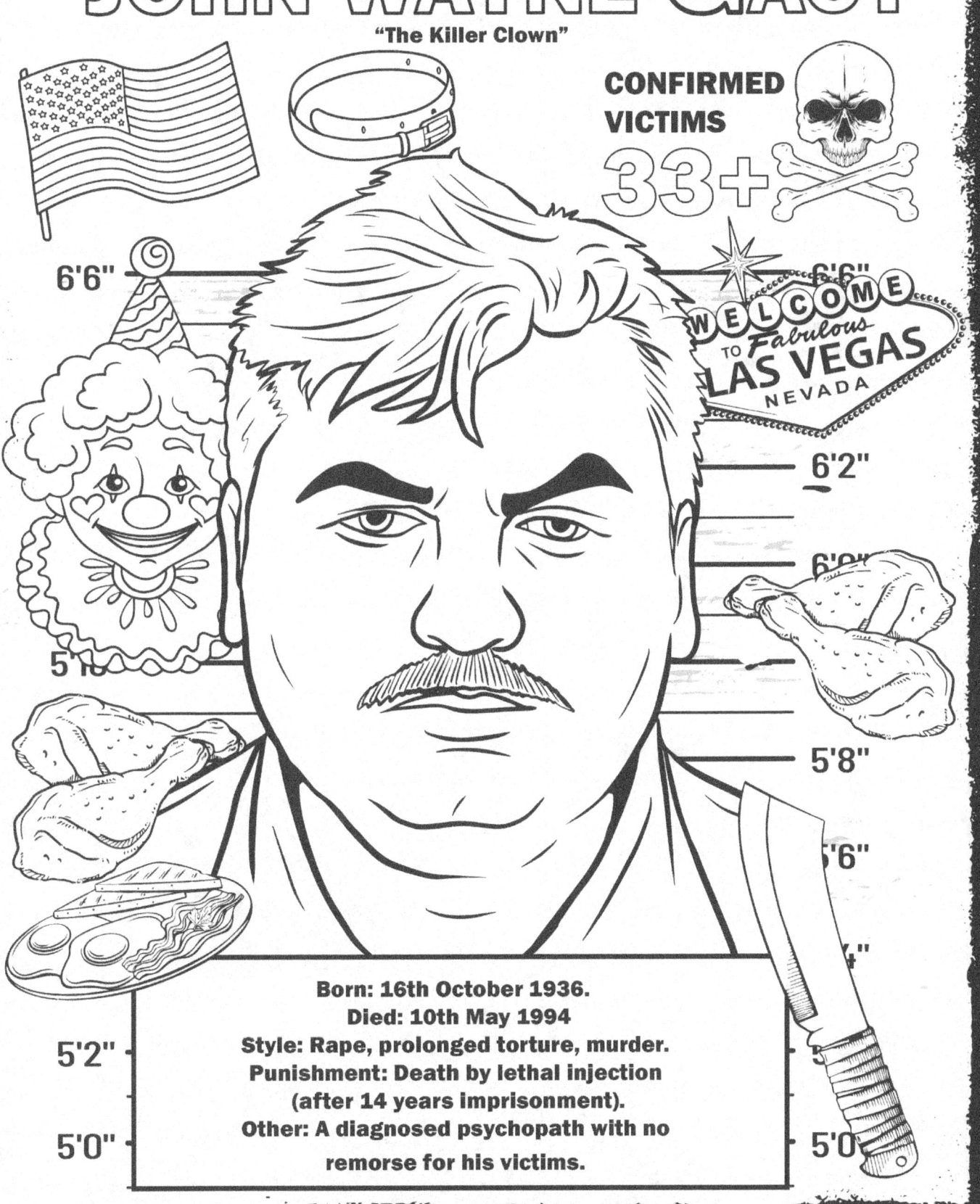

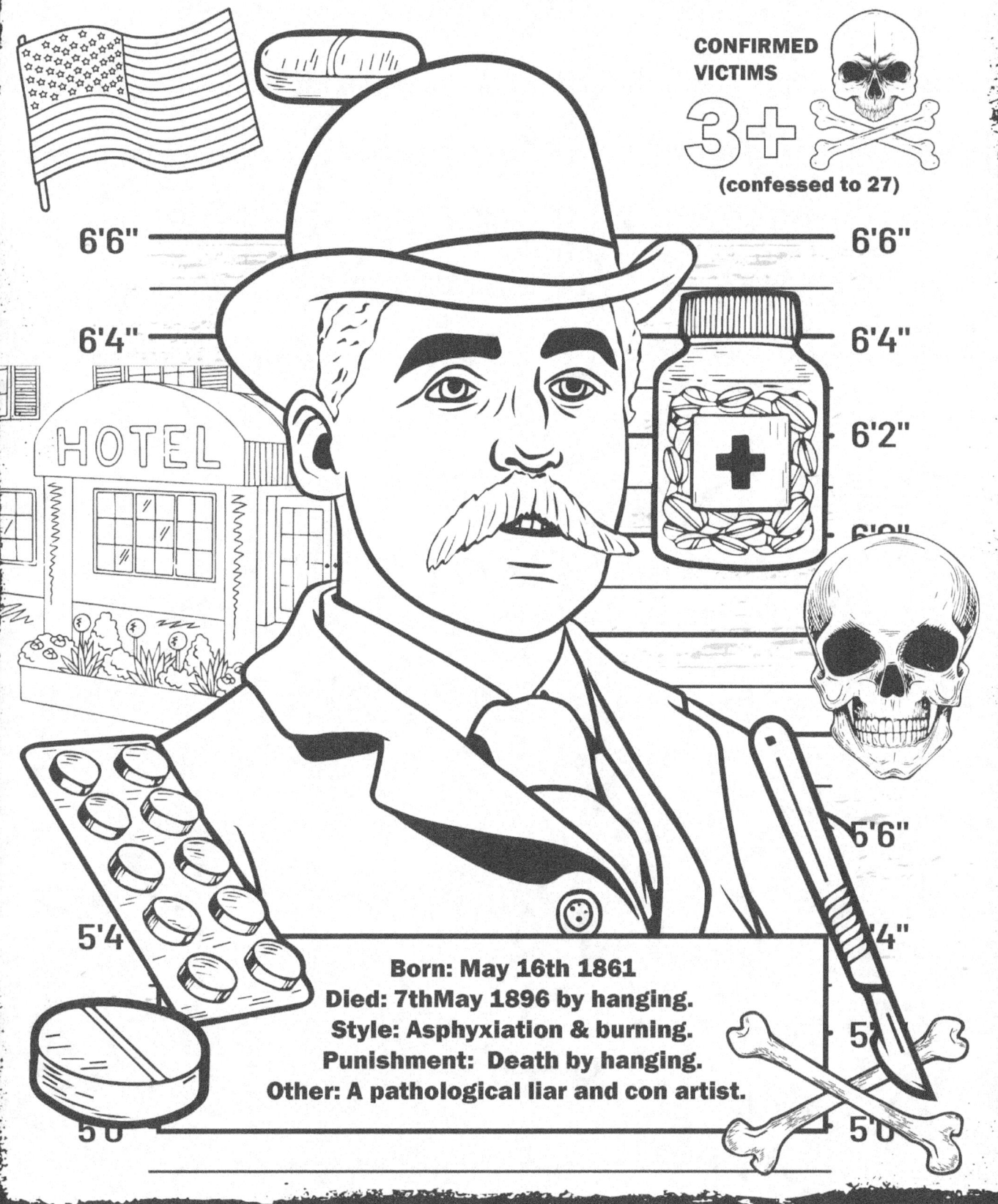

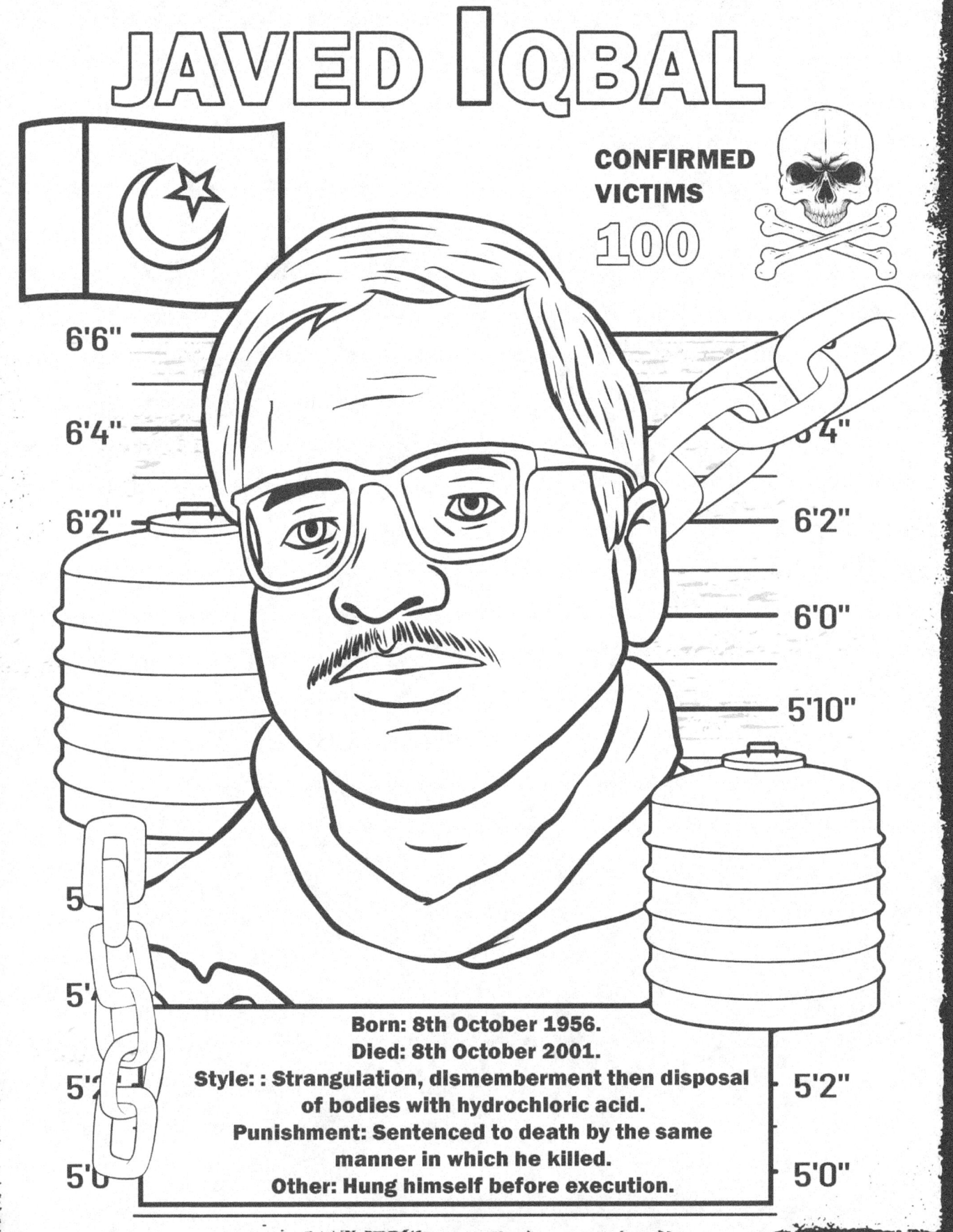

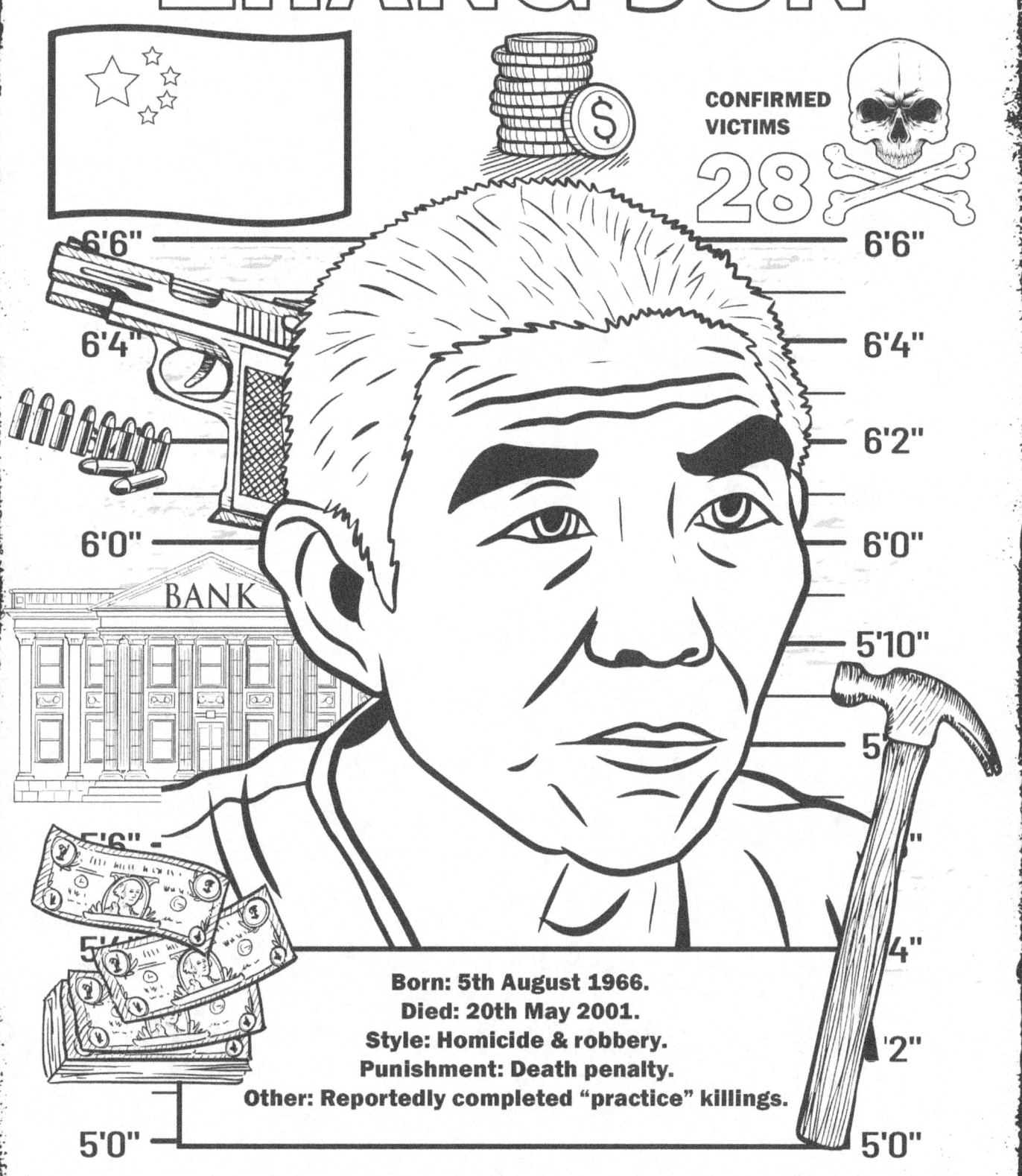

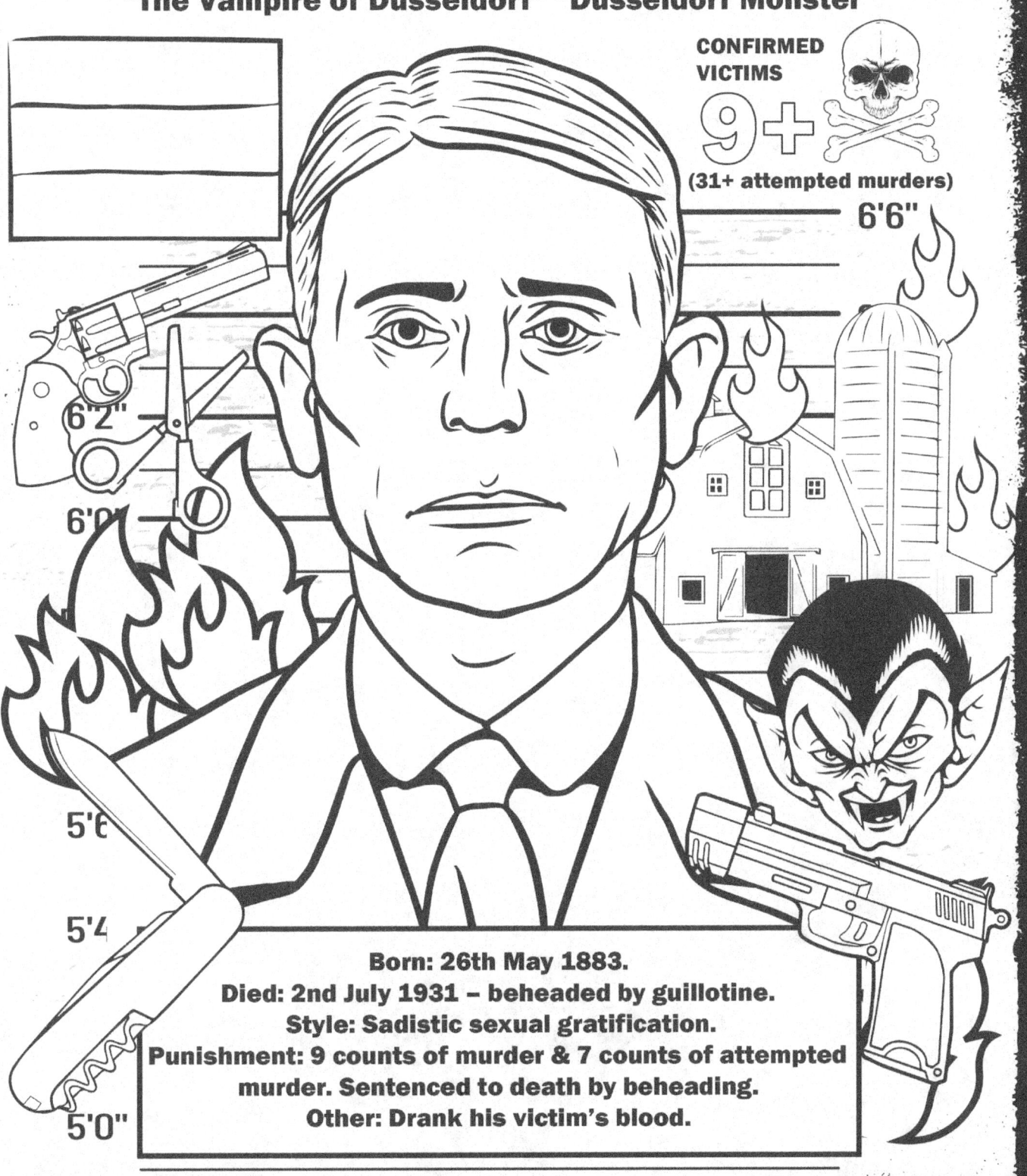

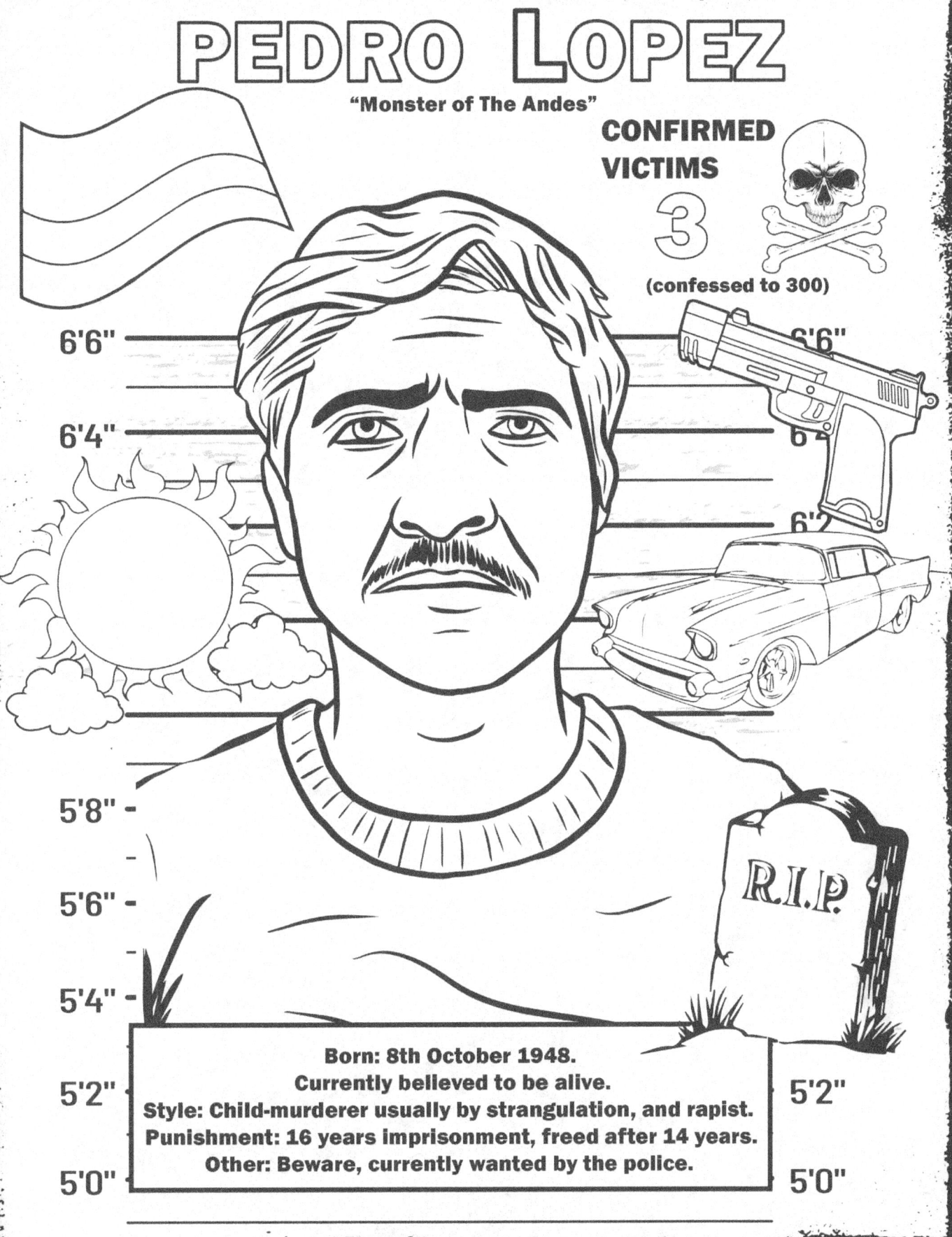

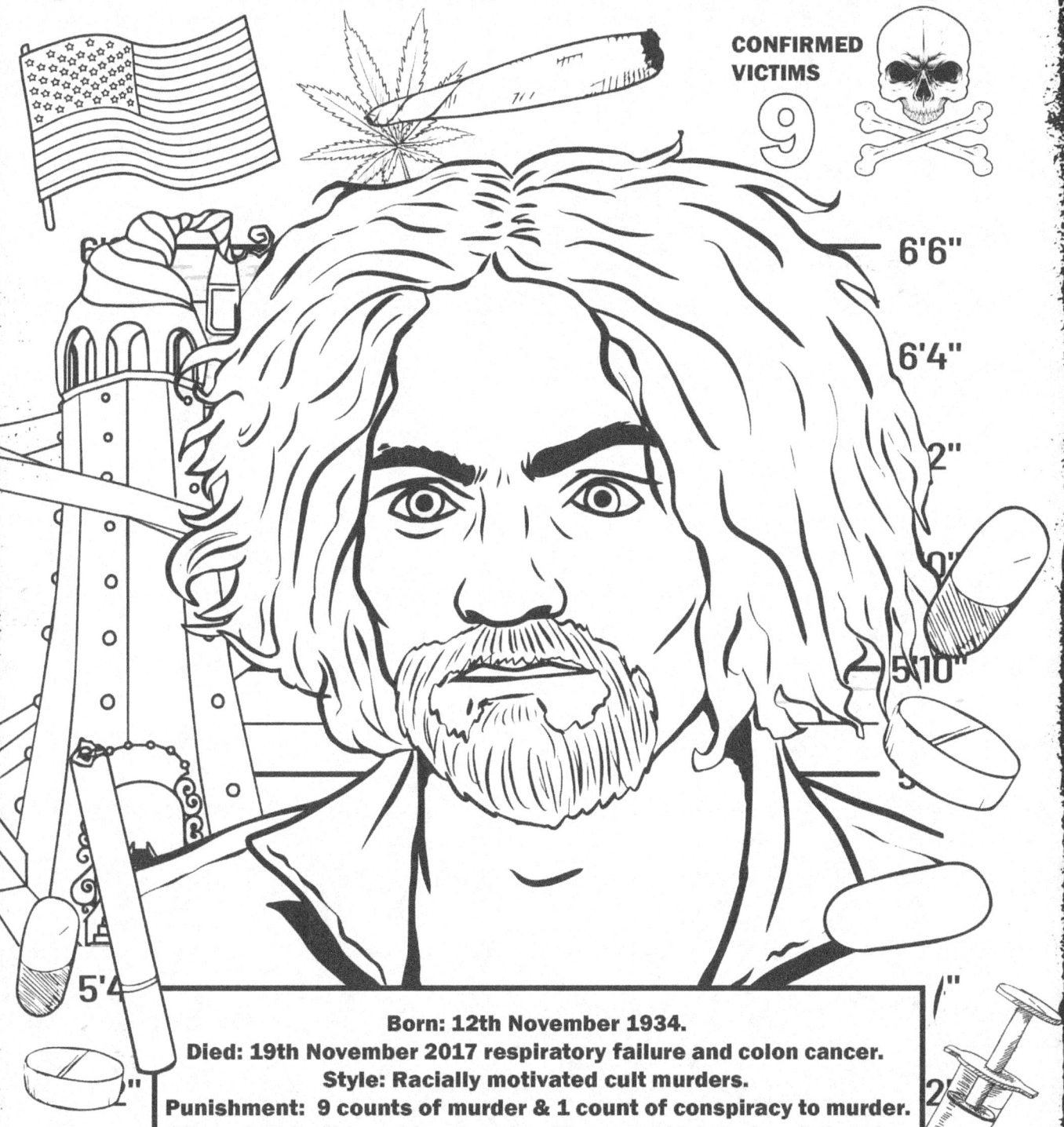

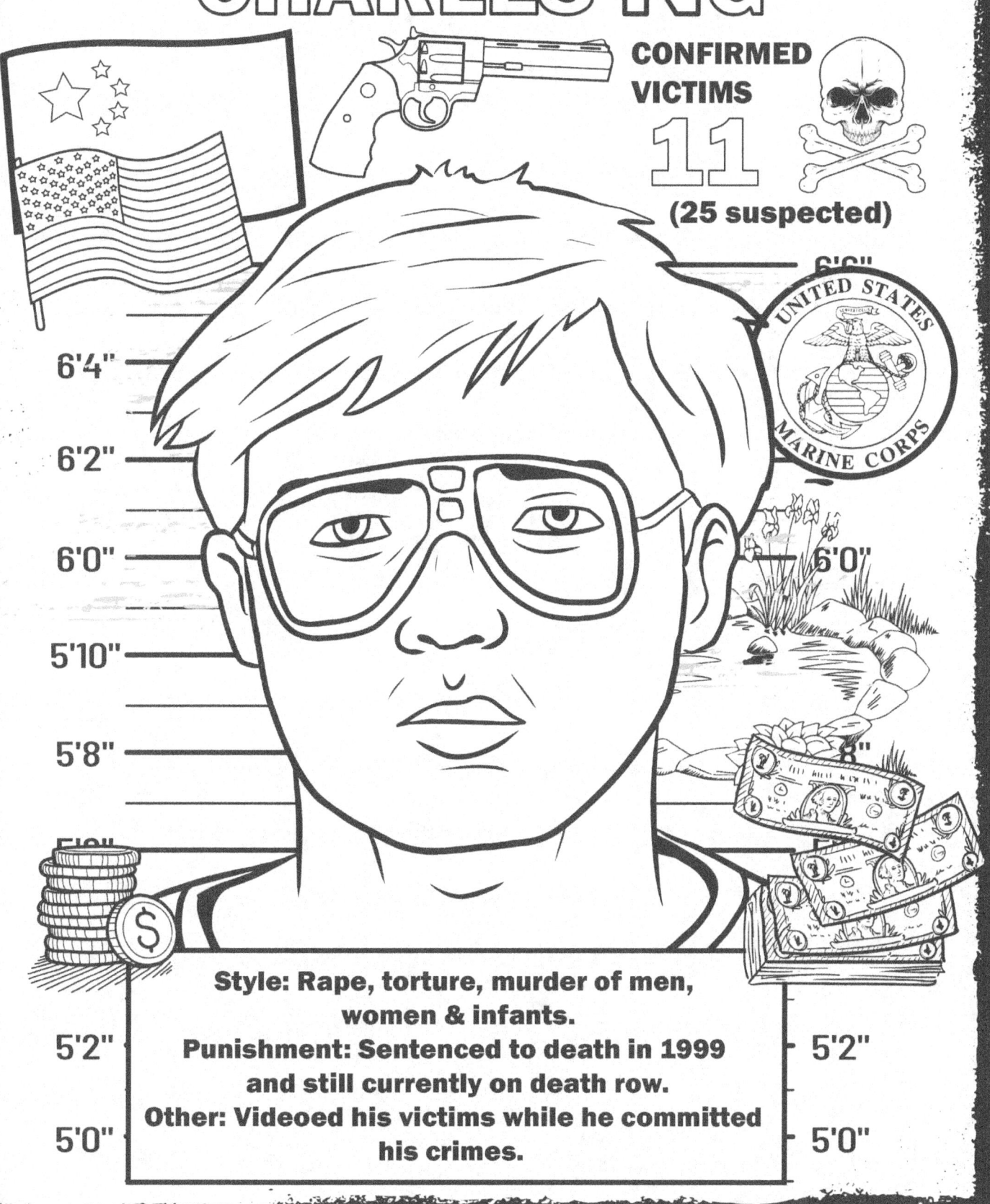

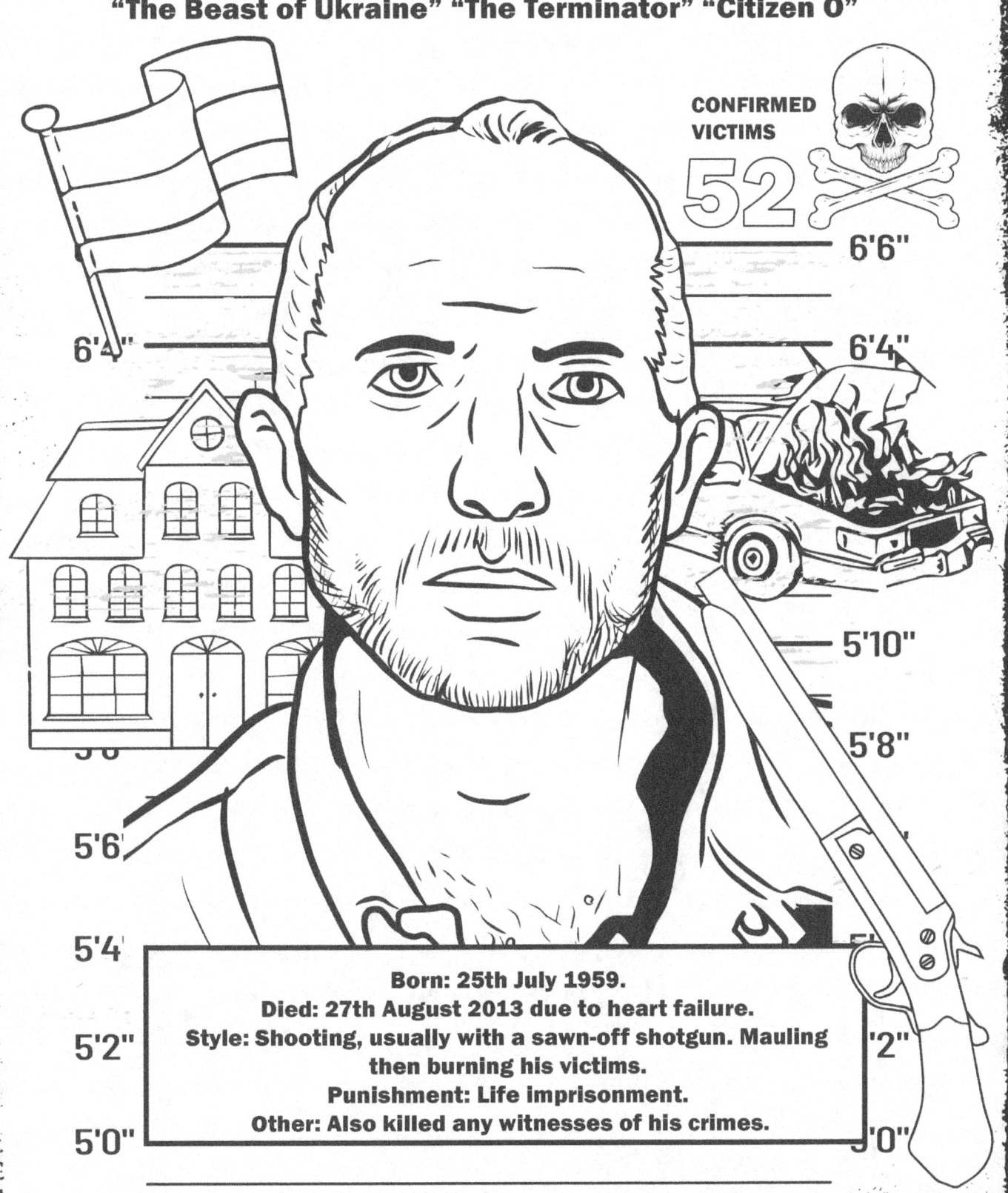

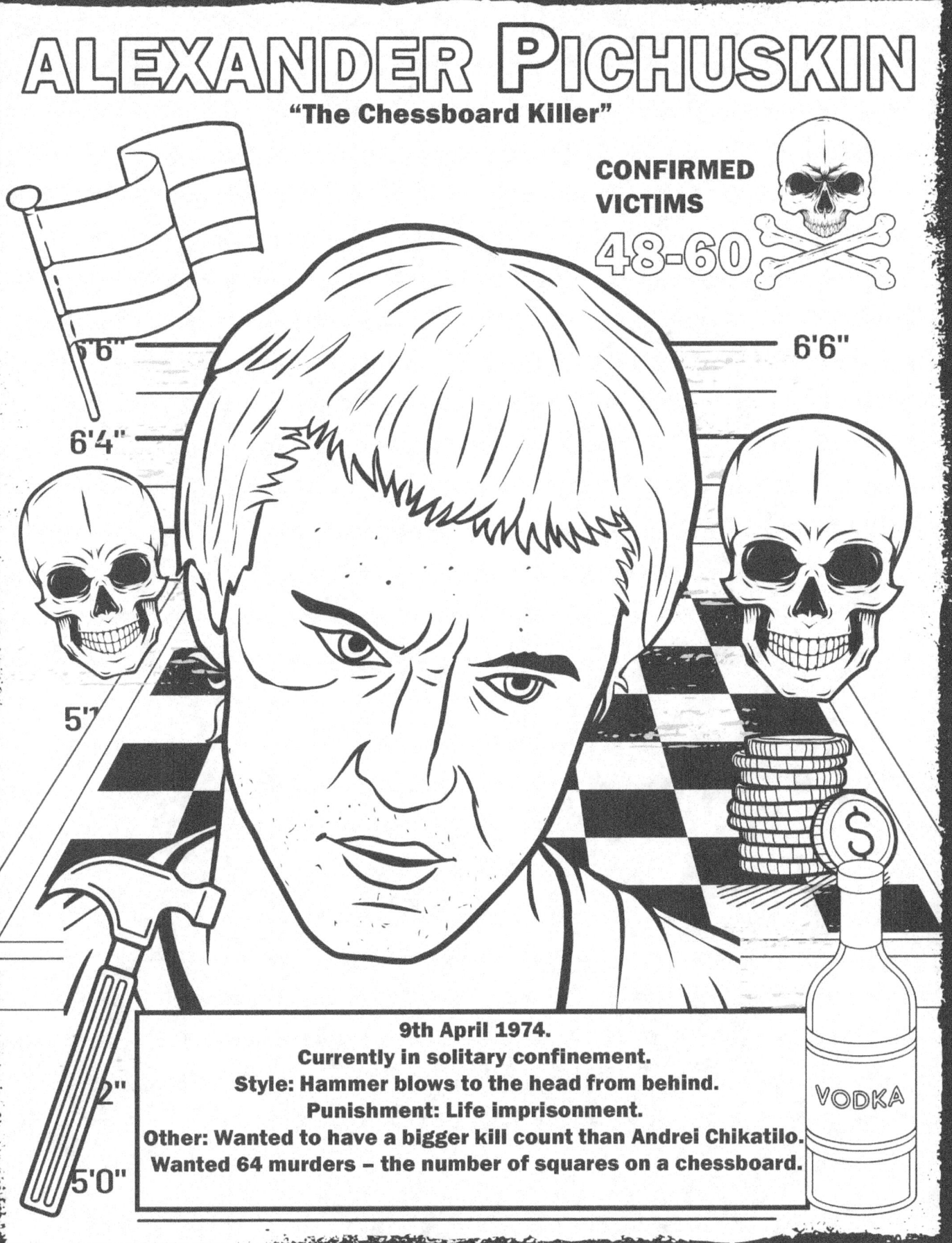

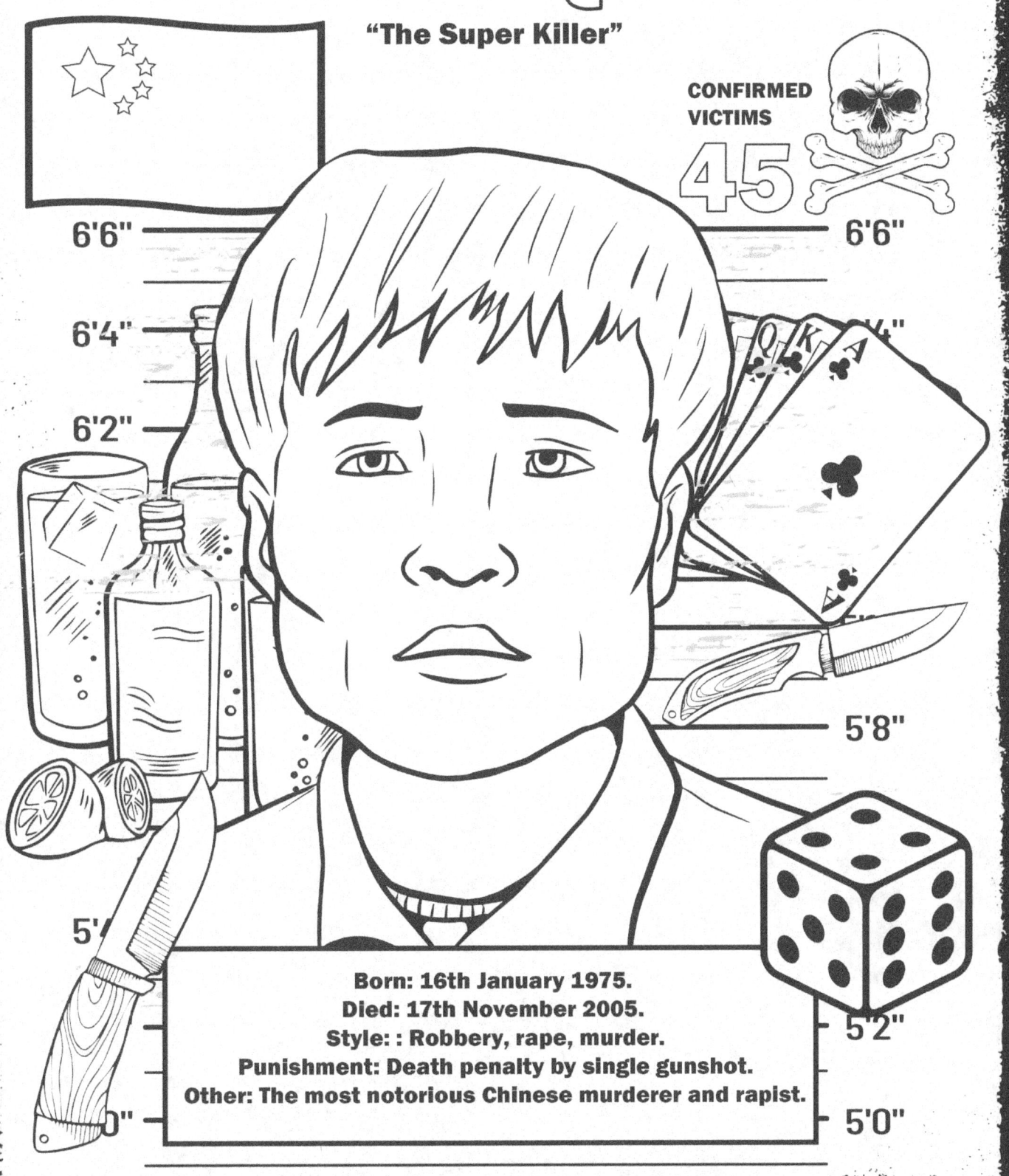

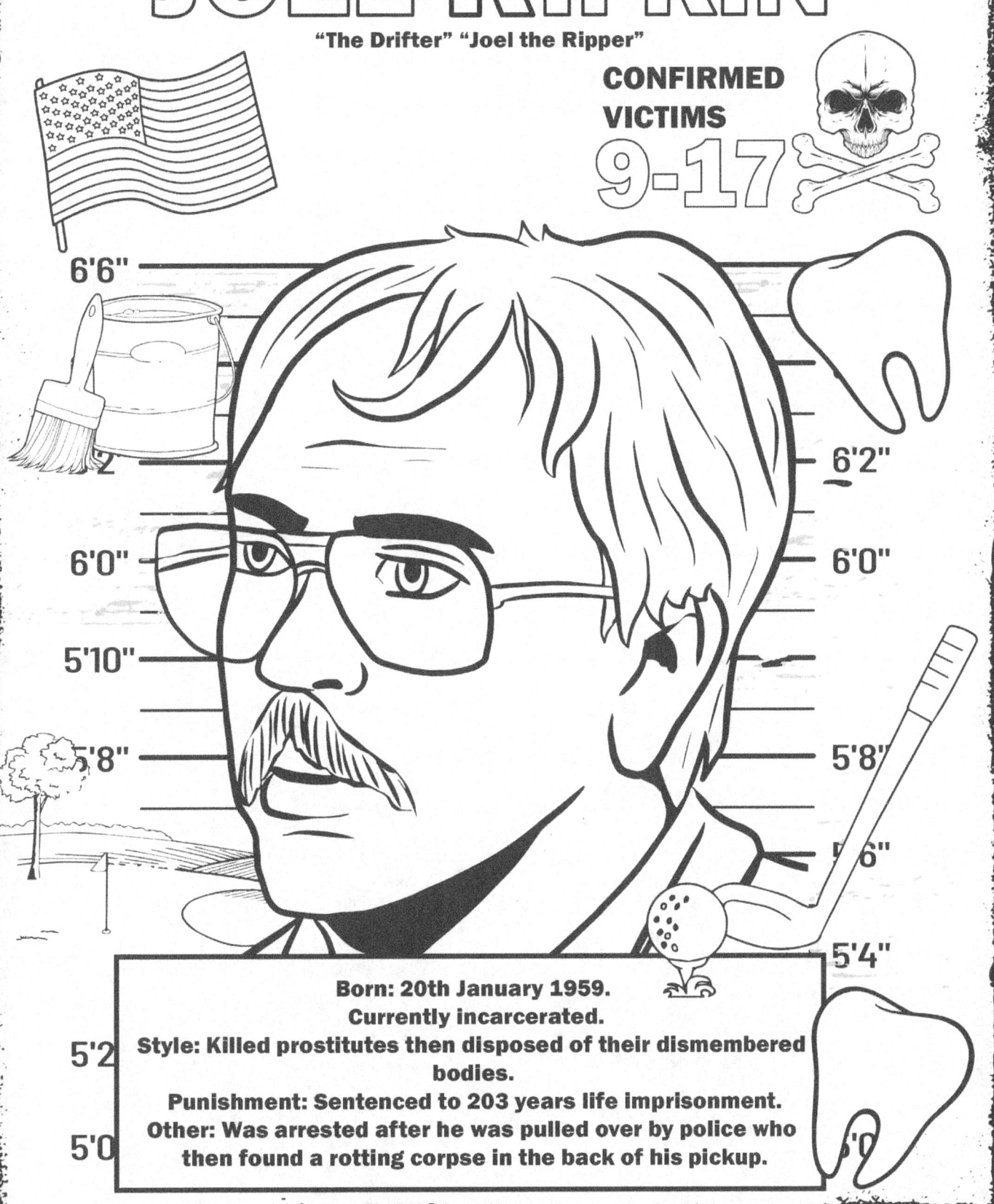

# HAROLD SHIPMAN

## "Dr. Death" "The Angel of Death" "The Good Doctor"

**CONFIRMED VICTIMS**
215
265+

CERTIFICATE OF DEATH

COUGH SYRYP

**Born:** 14th January 1946.
**Died:** 13th January 2004 (suicide while incarcerated).
**Style:** Administering lethal doses of diamorphine to elderly patients.
**Punishment:** Life imprisonment with a recommendation that he never be released.
**Other:** : The most prolific serial killer in modern day history.

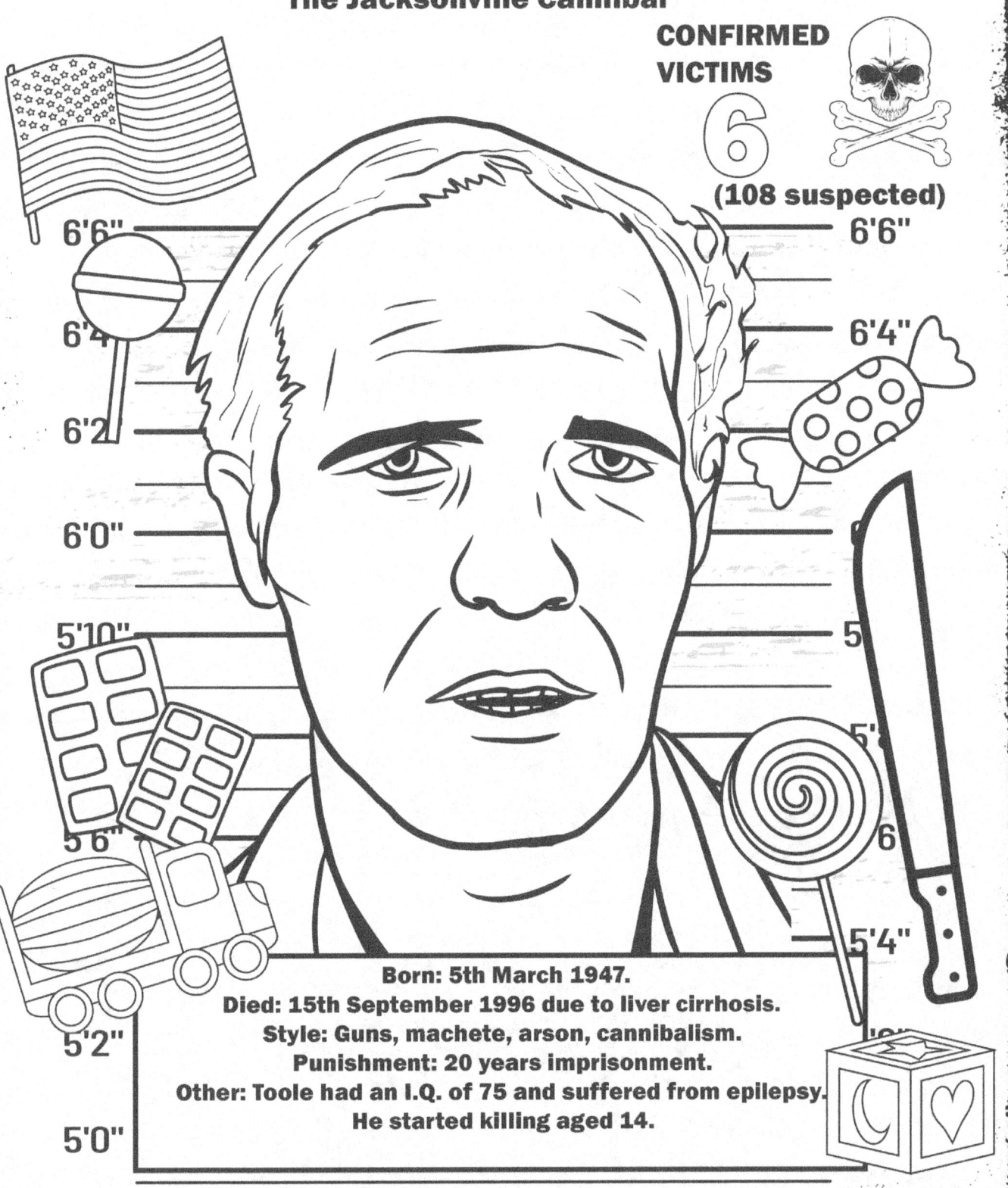

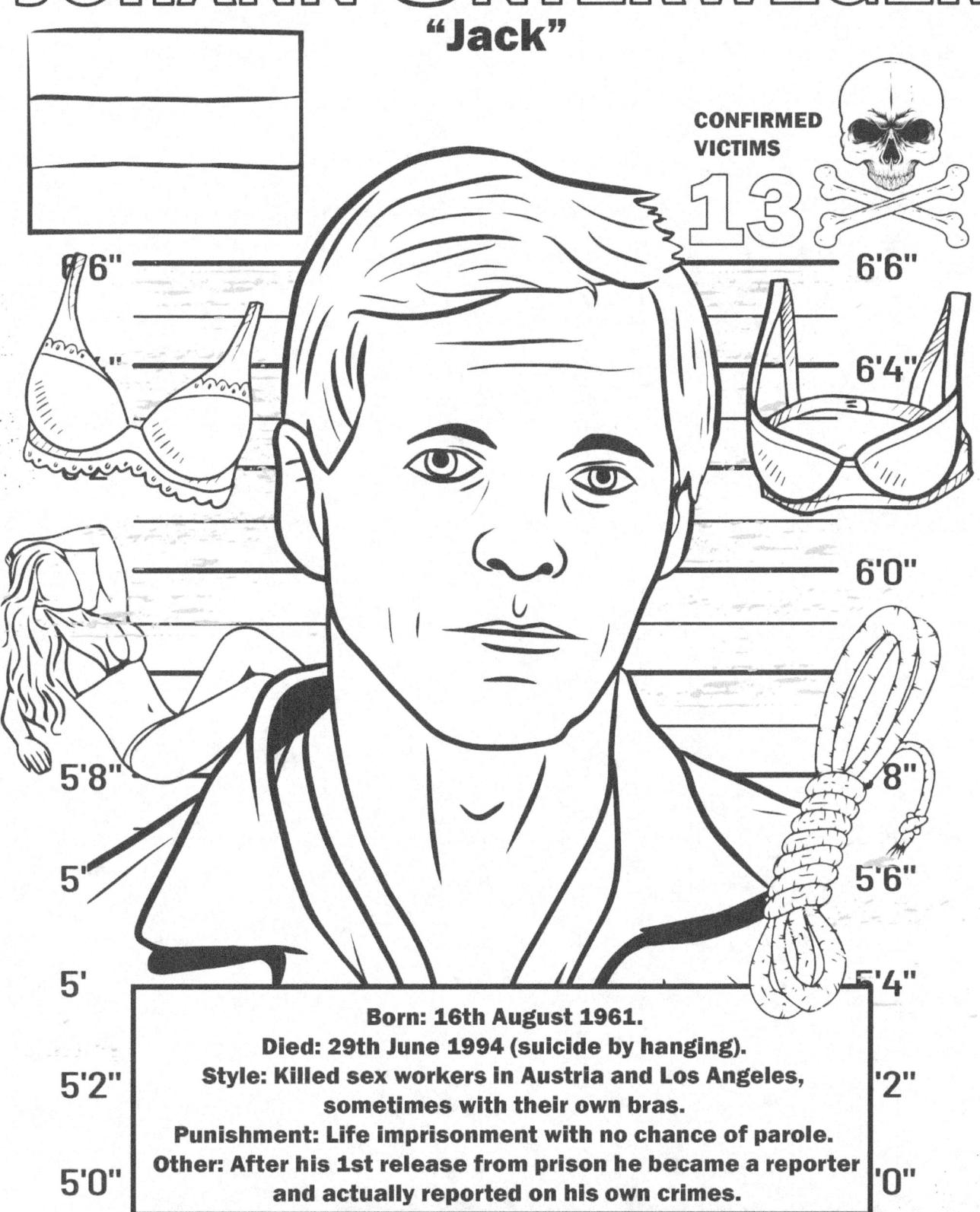

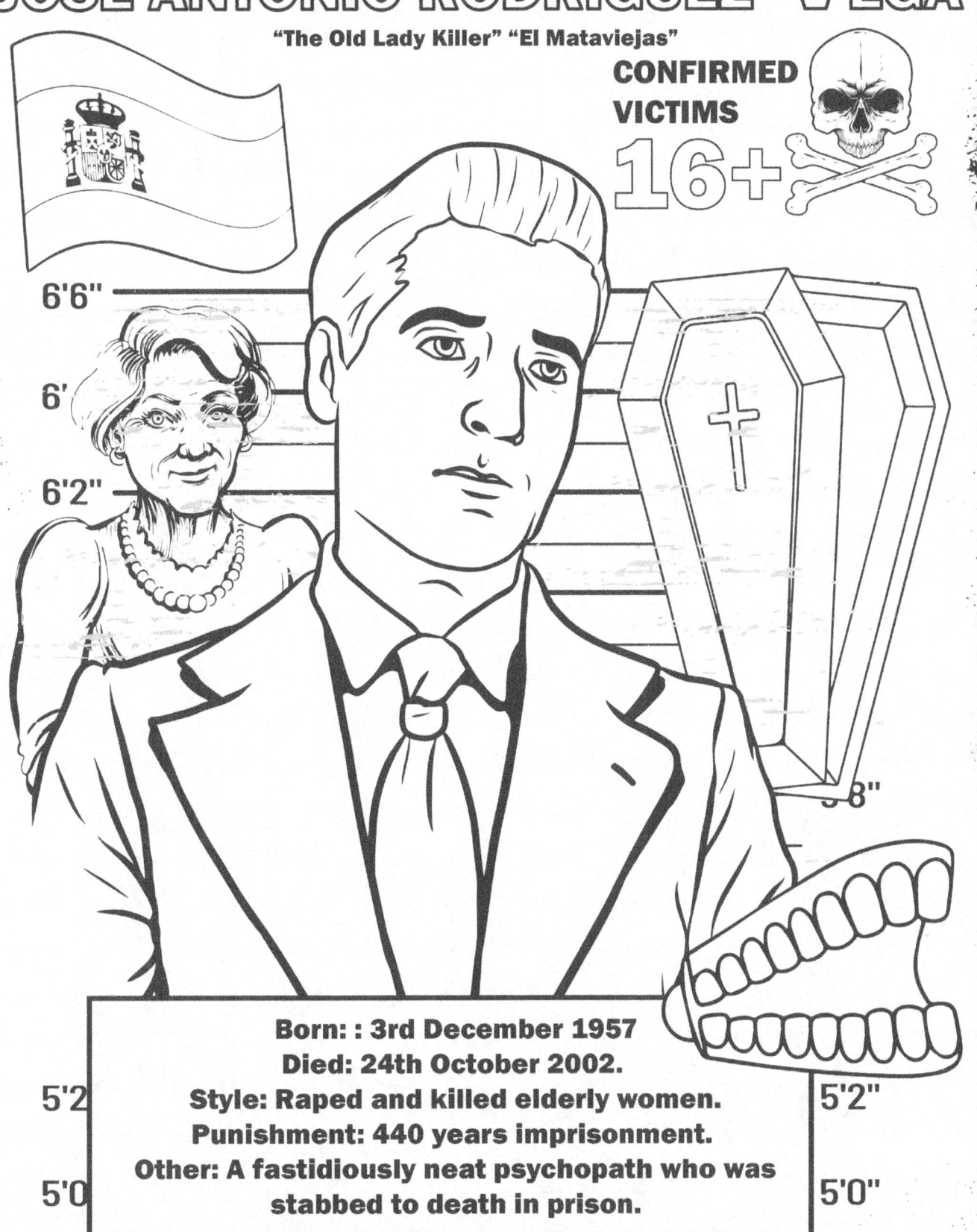

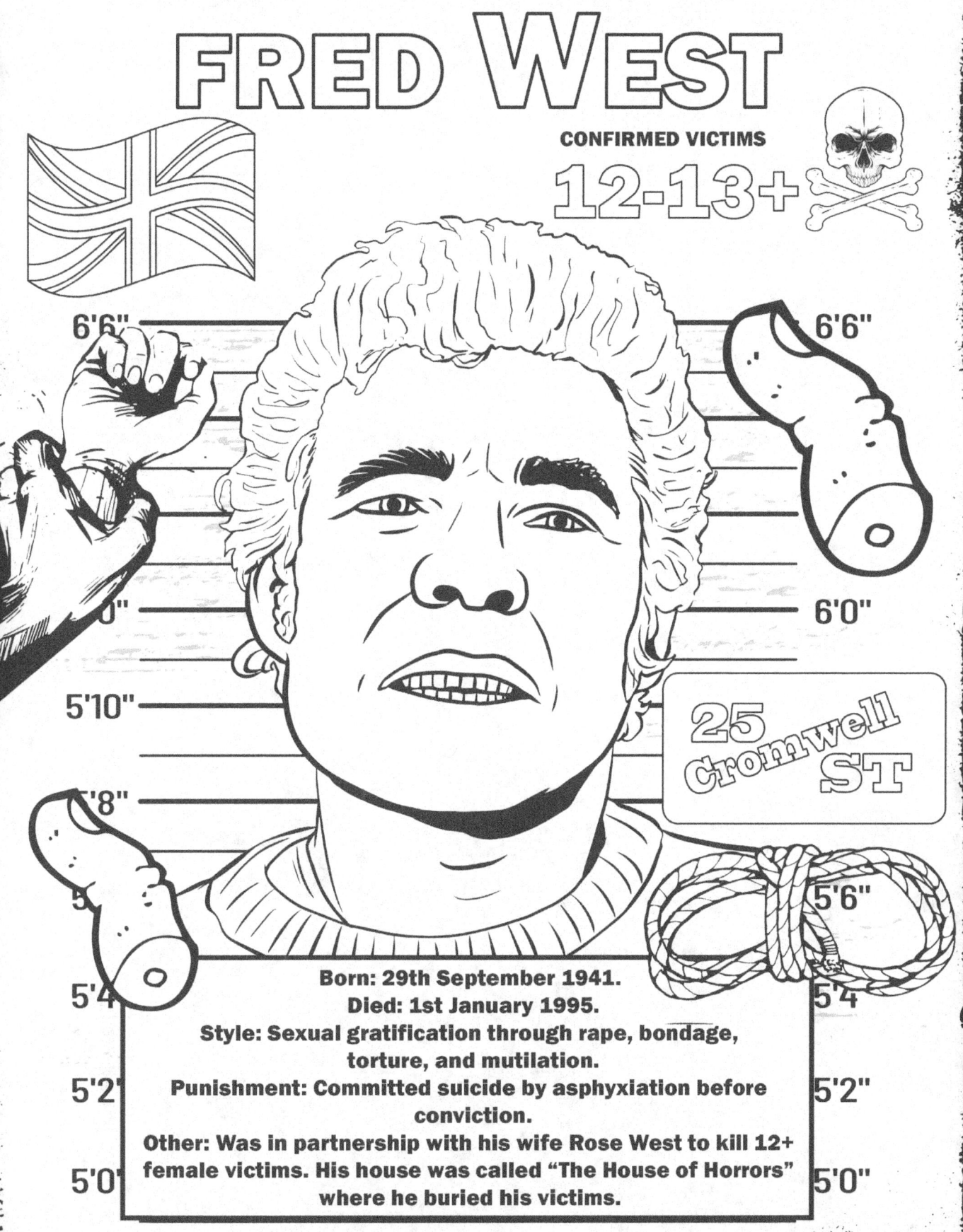

# YANG XINHAI

## "Monster Killer"

**CONFIRMED VICTIMS: 67**

Born: 29th July 1968.
Died: 14th February 2004 by firing squad.
Style: Killed several families with axes, shovels and hammers. Rape, murder.
Punishment: Death penalty.
Other: Believed to have the longest and most gruesome killing spree in Chinese history.

# Yoo Young-Chul
## "Raincoat Killer"

**CONFIRMED VICTIMS: 17**

**Born:** 18th April 1970.
**Died:** Currently incarcerated in Seoul prison.
**Style:** Broke into wealthy elderly citizens homes and bludgeoned them to death with a hammer. Killed sex workers too in same manner. Sometimes burned and ate his victims.
**Punishment:** Sentenced to death, but currently still incarcerated.
**Other:** He envied his wealthy victims due to his childhood poverty. He started hating women when his partner left him once she learnt of his crimes.

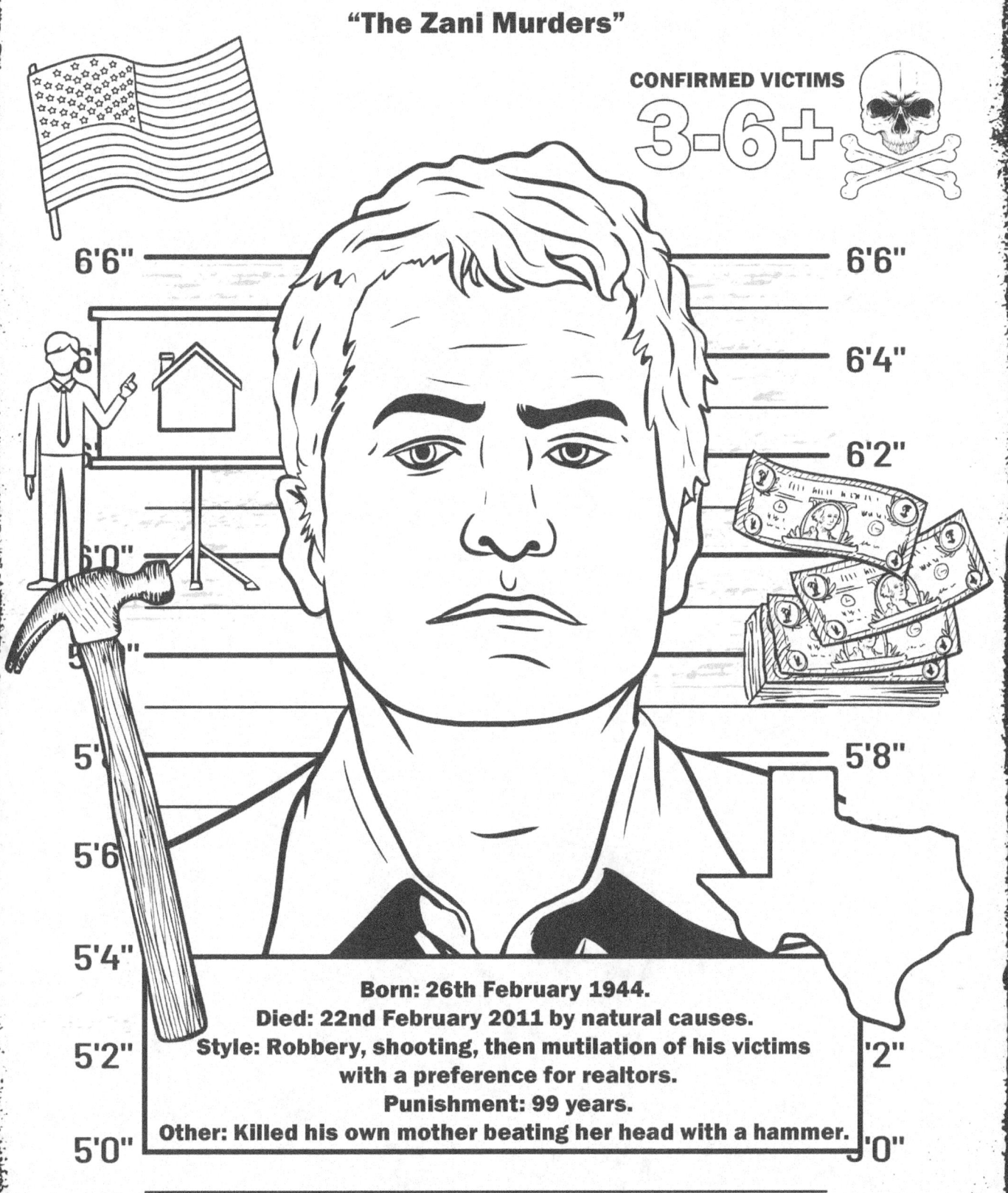

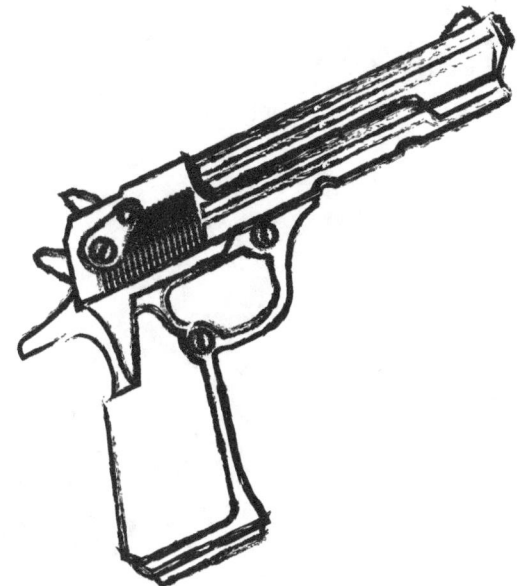
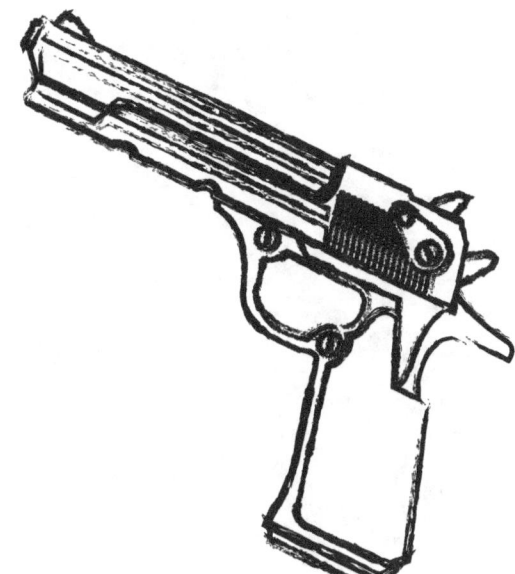

# Serial Killers Bonus Coloring Pages

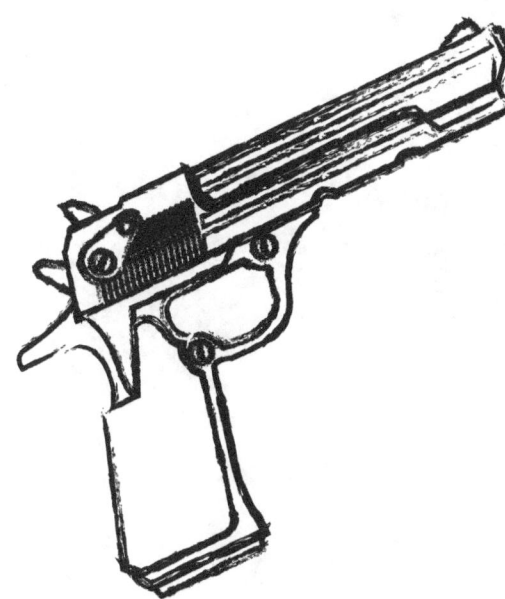
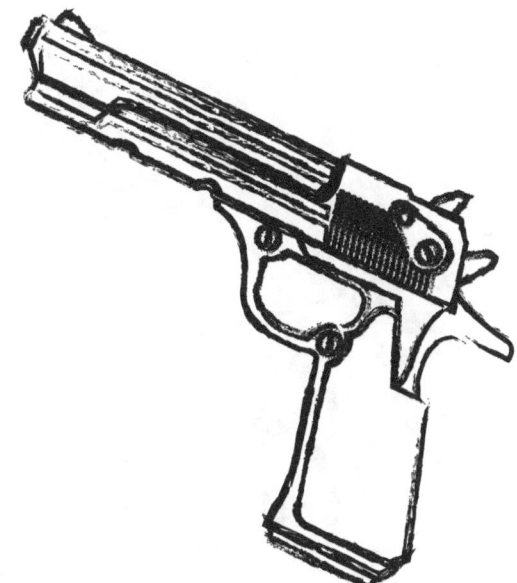

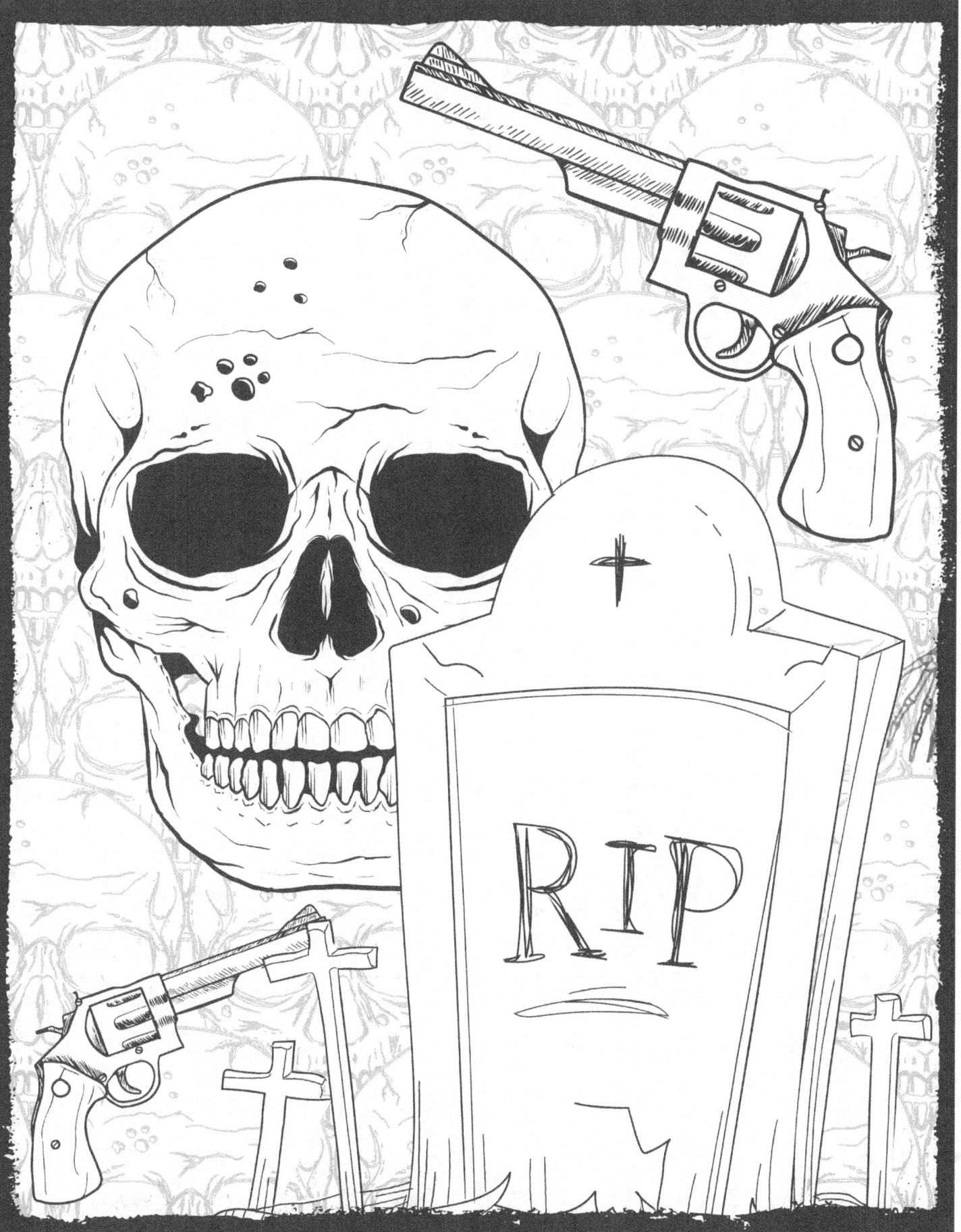

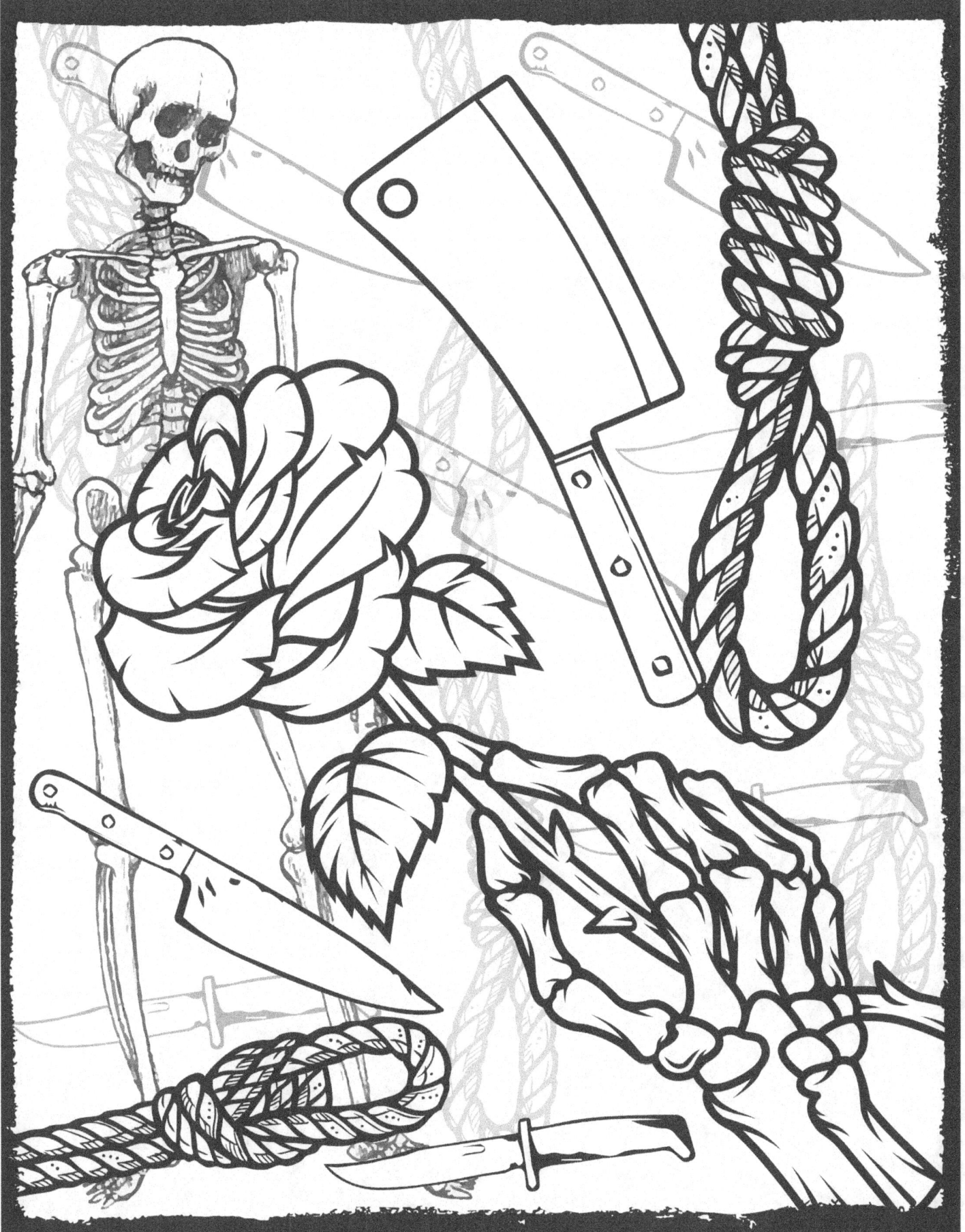

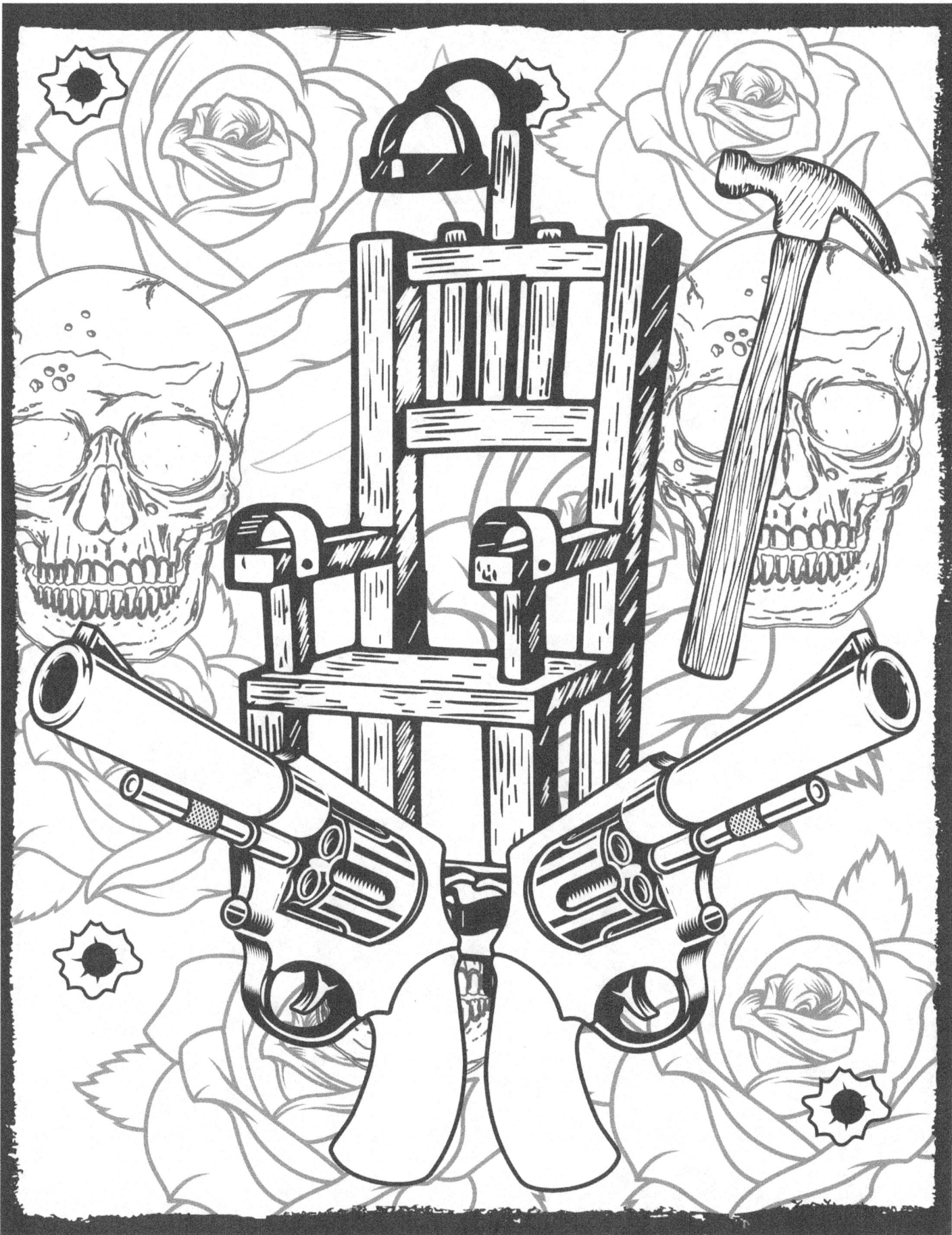

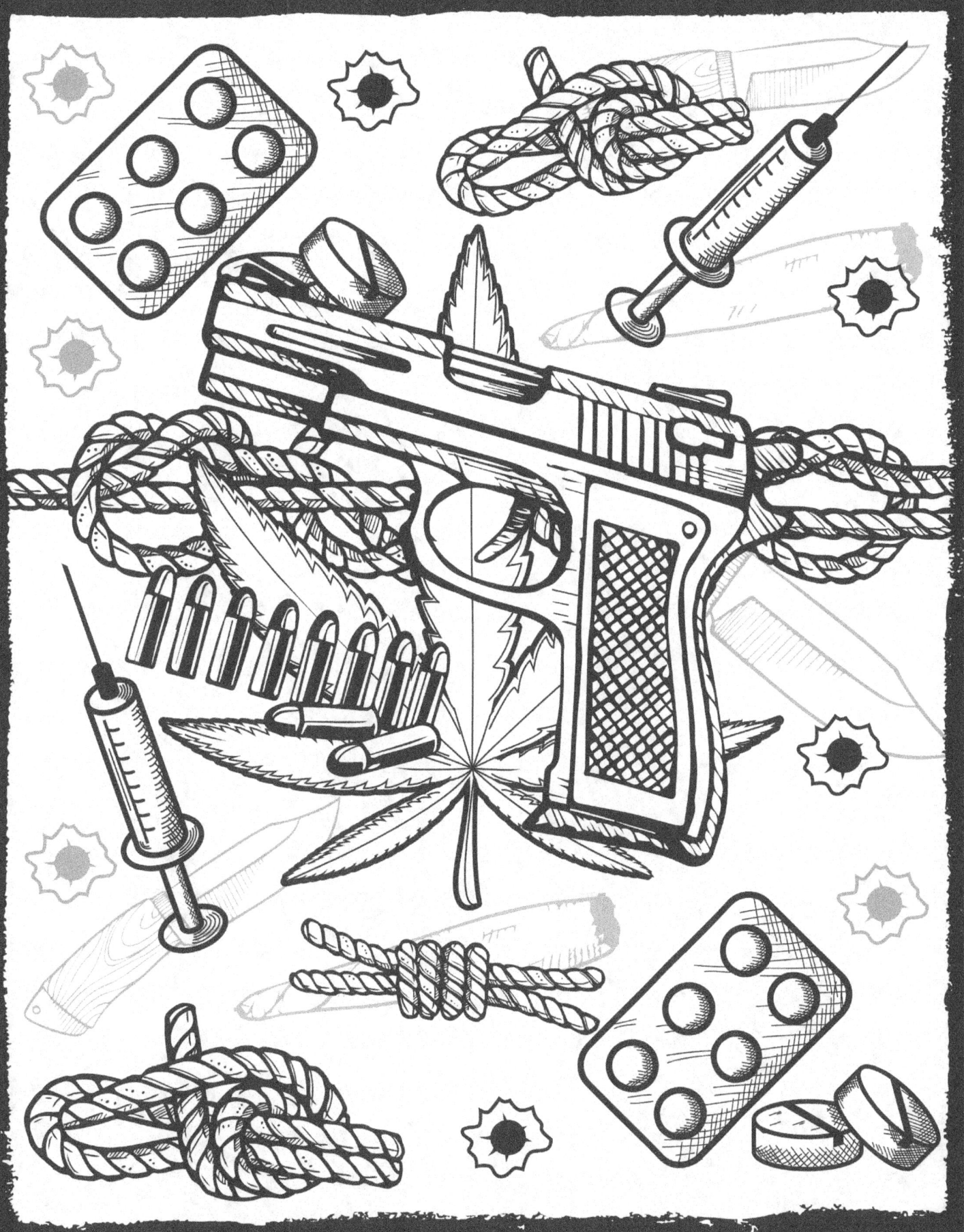

# A little favor please!

I really hope you enjoyed bringing to life your Serial Killer masterpieces and that you also managed to get some well-deserved stress reducing down-time whilst you were at it! I can't begin to imagine what it must have been like to be one of these killers or, even worse, one of their victims of course.

I really take pride in my work and strive to try and bring some fun and enjoyment into this sometimes difficult and challenging world in which we live. If you did get some pleasure from this book, I would really appreciate it if you could take a few moments to write an honest review to share your experience with others. This would help me keep doing what I love doing – and that's bringing a bit of fun to the world through our shared love of anything slightly 'unusual' – and the art of coloring of course!

Thanks so much and take care,

Kitty B xoxo

P.S. If you enjoyed this title, why don't you also check out my other books:

- **Cat Butt Coloring Book – Work From Home Edition.**

It's packed with our fun and amusing feline friends getting into all sorts of butt-based mischief!

US:    www.amazon.com/dp/B0875ZJNPC
UK:    www.amazon.co.uk/dp/B0875ZJNPC

Or, there's also my totally amazing drinking animals cocktail coloring book:

- **Drinking Animals Coloring Book - A fun & humorous adult coloring book with delicious cocktail recipes for pleasure, relaxation and stress relief.**

US: www.amazon.com/dp/B08B7DJFKJ
UK: www.amazon.co.uk/dp/B08B7DJFKJ

Or if you're feeling like you need to <u>really</u> let off some steam there's:

- **The Curious Healing Properties Of Coloring: A cheeky but relaxing alternative coloring book for adults.**

US: www.amazon.com/dp/B089D1G9GB
UK: www.amazon.co.uk/dp/B089D1G9GB

Please feel free to check them out too, you won't regret it. In fact, I think you'll like them quite a lot too.

## Please test your colors here:

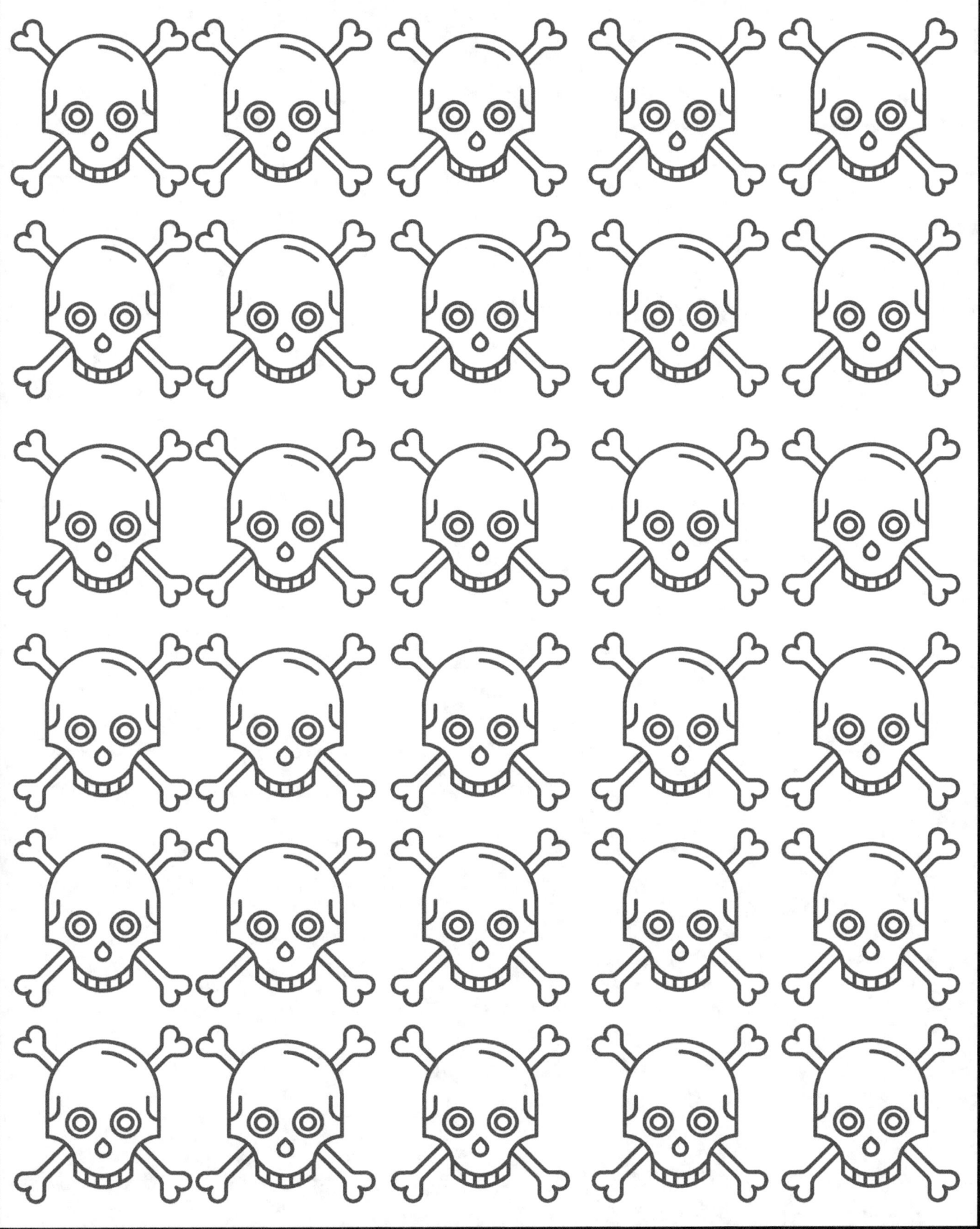

www.ingramcontent.com/pod-product-compliance
Lightning Source LLC
Chambersburg PA
CBHW080523220526
45465CB00006B/2572